The American Dream
for Students of Color

The American Dream for Students of Color

Myths and Barriers to Educational Success

Gretchen Givens Generett
and Amy M. Olson

LEXINGTON BOOKS
Lanham • Boulder • New York • London

Published by Lexington Books
An imprint of The Rowman & Littlefield Publishing Group, Inc.
4501 Forbes Boulevard, Suite 200, Lanham, Maryland 20706
www.rowman.com

6 Tinworth Street, London SE11 5AL, United Kingdom

Copyright © 2021 by The Rowman & Littlefield Publishing Group, Inc.

All rights reserved. No part of this book may be reproduced in any form or by any electronic or mechanical means, including information storage and retrieval systems, without written permission from the publisher, except by a reviewer who may quote passages in a review.

British Library Cataloguing in Publication Information Available

Library of Congress Cataloging-in-Publication Data

Names: Givens, Gretchen Zita, author. | Olson, Amy, author.
Title: The American dream for students of color : myths and barriers to educational success / Gretchen Givens Generett and Amy Olson.
Description: Lanham : Lexington Books, [2021] | Includes bibliographical references and index.
Identifiers: LCCN 2020057350 (print) | LCCN 2020057351 (ebook) | ISBN 9781793610973 (Cloth : acid-free paper) | ISBN 9781793610980 (ebook) | ISBN 9781793610997 (Pbk)
Subjects: LCSH: African Americans--Education. | Educational equalization--United States. | American Dream. | Mentoring in education. | Multicultural education. | Academic achievement--United States. | Racism in education. | Discrimination in education.
Classification: LCC LC2801 .G59 2021 (print) | LCC LC2801 (ebook) | DDC 370.89/96073--dc23
LC record available at https://lccn.loc.gov/2020057350
LC ebook record available at https://lccn.loc.gov/2020057351

Contents

Acknowledgments	vii
Prologue: Hard Work = Courage and Other Ways False Stories of Meritocracy are (Re)Told in Schools	ix
1 The Stories that Shaped Us	1
2 The Stories Educators Tell	23
3 The Stories Students Tell	51
4 Reframing the Stories We Tell	71
5 The Stories We Aspire to Tell	85
Bibliography	91
Index	97
About the Author	103

Acknowledgments

Sincere thanks and appreciation to the educators and students who shared their stories with us. We were humbled by your generosity and graciousness with your time, honesty, and profound insight. We continue to be encouraged by your hard work, perseverance, and courage to go beyond expectations, and we are eternally grateful for your commitment to education.

We have the pleasure of working with amazing graduate students! To Triantafyllia Sarri, thank you for the research, coding, and presenting that you did in support of this work. To Carol Schoenecker, thank you for proofreading the final draft and for your thoughtful and insightful questions. To Ramona Crawford, thank you for the research, coding, and presenting that you did for us. And special thanks to Ramona for the last-minute switch from APA to Chicago Style and for the cover art. Fillia, Carol, and Ramona, we are so blessed to have you in our lives.

DEDICATION

Gretchen—This book is dedicated to my grandmothers, Florence Wyche Stith and Lena Mason Givens. While no longer physically with me, the stories you shared about love, courage, strength, hard work, and perseverance continue to sustain me.

Amy—This book is dedicated to my grandmothers and great-grandmothers: Muriel Gene and Betty Louise for stories always bookended by hugs, Minnie Agnes and Sophie Wanda for stories told over dress-up and warm meals, and Josephine Ethel and Ruth Ethel for stories passed down. You taught me the everyday courage in working hard, loving hard, and loving to work hard.

Prologue

Hard Work = Courage and Other Ways False Stories of Meritocracy are (Re)Told in Schools

We are completing this book from our respective homes as we enter the second month of reduced face to face occupancy in classrooms with students joining online at the university due to COVID-19. The semester includes daily health screenings and updates of the number of COVID-19 cases in our region and in our children's school district. We are besieged by verdicts and political commentary that fuel the flames of racism as a Summer of protest against systemic racism, turns into a Fall of protests. We could not have imagined what our lives would be like, let alone feel like, when we packed our belongings and left campus on March 13, 2020. We share this reality to provide a framing of our reality as we complete this book. Our current reality is drastically different from where we were four years ago when we began this work. Conversations about the research in this book began in 2016 set against the backdrop of a Leadership Symposium designed as a Community Learning Exchange (CLE). Wanting to work together on a project that would inspire and sustain us both, we began talking. We talked at length about the debilitating forces of systems that perpetuated racial and class inequities in a city that had been voted "most livable city" for two consecutive years. In our conversations about livability, we asked "for whom" and connected the narrative of viable living options to schools, excellence, and success. With documented employment, education, and safety advantages, supported by a wide range of social, political, and economic institutions, our city should have little need to explore the intergenerational transmission of inequalities at work within communities in our city. Yet, an in-depth analysis by the Center for Race and Social Problems, conducted by the University of Pittsburgh's School of Social Work in 2015, clearly demonstrates that the city is not safe, affordable, or kid-friendly for nearly one half of its residents, who lack equality of educational opportunity, stability, and social mobility.

Our discussions turned toward educators and the challenges that they face addressing inequities in a city whose narrative consists of being "the most livable city." We wondered about the stories teachers told their students whose lives take place in the shadows of the most livable city.

What did they tell students about the disparities that plagued their city? In asking these questions, we began to share stories of individual educators who, despite evidence that their system was failing some of their most vulnerable students and that their work was not valued, continued to work against the grain as they battled systemic inequities in their school buildings. Our discussions led us to the topic of courage, and we asked, "why and how do educators find the courage to act upon injustice and inequities?"

While COVID-19 has upended our lives as we know it, this global pandemic has also exposed, in more vivid ways, the inequities that plague the systems that we have created and how those inequities continue to devalue the lives of historically underserved, under-resourced, and underrepresented groups in the United States. According to the CDC website on September 26, 2020, "race and ethnicity are risk markers for other underlying conditions that impact health—including socioeconomic status, access to health care, and increased exposure to the virus due to occupation (e.g., frontline, essential, and critical infrastructure workers)" (https://www.cdc.gov/coronavirus/2019-ncov/covid-data/investigations-discovery/hospitalization-death-by-race-ethnicity.html). Disturbing data is also evident in education. As school districts pushed learning online, it was clear that the educational disparities that already existed between students of color and their White peers would increase. As a result of the COVID-19, many parents of vulnerable students have lost jobs and face housing insecurity. For students who are doing online school or hybrid formats, the lack of reliable internet or a device to work on correlates into fewer hours of class time (Center for American Progress, 2020). According to the Center for American Progress, "While the short- and long-term impacts of coronavirus-related school closures and job losses on children's educational outcomes cannot be measured yet, it is already clear that there are differential effects by race on access to educational resources as a result of the pandemic" (https://www.americanprogress.org/issues/race/news/2020/08/12/489260/black-white-wealth-gap-will-widen-educational-disparities-coronavirus-pandemic/).

The negative effects of the pandemic and racial unrest cannot be understated. As faculty in a School of Education, who teach and study disparities in the field, we are all too familiar with the pervasiveness of and the debilitating impact of disparities on schools prior to the coronavirus (Darder 1991; Giroux 1988; Kumashiro 2000). In certain educational spaces we did not think that educational disparities could get worse and yet, this pandemic demonstrates that things can get worse as it continues to highlight the insidiousness of the effects of systemic inequities on schools. Like before the pandemic, teachers struggle to serve students from underserved, under-resourced, and historically marginalized groups. Today this struggle persists as teachers become essential workers who are called upon to work despite risk to their health and that of their families. They have had to transition their work online and to continue to meet the diverse needs of students all while wearing masks and face shields. Still other educators are teaching blended classes where some students are physically in class while others log in online. They are working to support parents who struggle to assist their children with ongoing changes as they try to adjust to our new normal as well. Like the narrative of the "most livable city," while disparities were plentiful, we wonder what stories will be told about schools during the coronavirus, about the educators working in them, and the youth and families that they serve. We share this context to illustrate that while educational disparities are increasing in schools nationwide, this moment will one day be history and we will tell stories about what happened in education in 2020. We wonder what stories will be told?

ONE
The Stories that Shaped Us

We center stories in this book. Specifically, we examine tenets of the American Dream as a merit narrative enacted in schools to better understand how beliefs about talent, hard work, and perseverance support the status quo rather than critical analysis of barriers to educational success for students of color and students in poverty. Using narrative methodologies, we explore the surprising connections and consistencies within and between our personal narratives and the narratives of school youth and educators that work with them. Based on analysis of these shared stories, we argue for the importance of moving from individualized success stories that reify hard work and perseverance to collective, communal stories that serve to break down myths of meritocracy, critically examine inequities, and move educational advocates forward in authentic, audacious, hopeful work.

In this first chapter we outline the origins of this work and delve into our individual stories. In rendering our stories, we highlight how success and excellence, as a product of hard work and perseverance, is embedded in the fiber of our identities and we introduce how the power of the American Dream and the potency of the myth of meritocracy shapes our stories. We also share how family and school stories functioned in our lives to promote the perceived cause and effect relationships among the values of hard work, effort, and perseverance, and economic success in our minds and hearts through educational practices that focused on us as individuals and not the broken systems that we survived. After sharing our stories, we look back at them as a collection in an effort to better understand why sharing them with you is the first step to becoming aware of the salience of the meritocracy narrative in our individual stories across different time periods, cultures, and United States contexts. We believe that by looking at them as a collective, we set the stage for what the educators and students that we interviewed face in schools today.

THE BACK STORY

Our conversations began due to our proximity to each other in our academic department and grew because of the philosophical connections between our research agendas. Gretchen is an interdisciplinary scholar in the foundations of education whose research interrogates how class, race, racism, and power impact the educational experiences of students, teachers, and their communities. Her scholarship starts with self-narrative and portraiture that interrogates her educational experiences as a young girl schooled in suburban Richmond, yet tethered to her grandmother's front porch in rural Virginia. Blending the arts and sciences in her methodology, she uses stories to capture the complex, dynamic, and multifaceted ways in which race, class, and gender shape relationships to schooling. Her teaching suggests that reflective and interactive storytelling serves a function in uncovering and recovering our individual and collective stories so that we can be intentional in our efforts to not reproduce systemic inequities.

Amy self identifies as a teacher scholar, and as such her scholarship meaningfully influences her pedagogy. She is committed to improving the lived experiences of students. As a scholar, she explores how educator beliefs about content and what it means to learn and be successful in the classroom influence student outcomes. Her designs tend toward mixed methods wherein she uses contextualized qualitative work to support, critique, and provide rich description of the findings from more quantitative approaches. She often uses quantitative items such as surveys or assessments as an initial, structuring experience (e.g., see Coffey & Atkinson 1996) that allows participants to engage in deeper reflection and storytelling in follow-up qualitative data collection.

Standing in each other's offices we shared stories about our individual research and community work with teachers and educational leaders. In our respective teaching and research, we recognized that there are educators we have come to know whose pedagogical approaches to justice and equity are visceral and their actions to address inequities came without a lot of thought. For these educators, injustice and inequities in their schools were obvious as opposed to subtle and these injustices garnered emotional responses that led to actions to address them. Similarly, we recognized that these educators do equity work despite risk to their professional careers and without evidence that what they do will change inequities within the larger educational system. From our different entries into research, we each landed on similar questions—What about these particular educators made them fight for justice and equity on behalf of their students? What made them persist despite evidence that what they do will not make a difference? In doorways and hallways of our building, we wondered out loud how these teachers became the educators that they were today for their students and the communities that they serve. During those conversations we began to wonder out loud whether or not these particular educators were more courageous than other educators and if so, how did they get that way?

In asking these questions about courage and teaching, we shared the stories that frame our individual schooling and education as well as how these stories shape our work—stories of hard work and perseverance. We also shared the stories we heard in our school contexts and how we internalized or fought against those stories. We realized that, despite being different and growing up in very different contexts, we heard similar family and school stories. As researchers do, we began to delve into the power of stories to shape schooling and asked each other, "What stories about success and excellence are being told in schools today?" As we continued our discussions we circled back to our individual research on justice and equity work in schools and began to interrogate the social justice implications of school-based meritocracy narratives and how these narratives impact teachers' practice and students' identity development. Our conversations had come full circle. Equity, courage, narratives, excellence, and success, what are the connections?

Moral Courage and Storytelling

Across disciplines, courage is consistently admired because it is grounded in self-sacrifice, serves the needs of others, and is needed to enact all of the other virtues (Koerner 2014). Koerner identifies three critical components of courage within the literature. Citing interdisciplinary scholarship, she concludes that courage consists of addressing a morally worthy goal and taking an intentional action despite the perceived risks, threats, or obstacles. It takes courage to be authentic in educational systems that are "characterized by fear, the denial of individuality, and the affirmation of conformity" (Goldenberg 1978, 8). As early as the nineteenth century, philosophers defined moral courage as the willingness for an individual to confront "the pain and dangers of social disapproval in the performance of what they believe to be duty" (Sidgewick 1913, 333, quoted in Press 2018). Moral courage is most often associated with actions in the service of others or the communal good, but researchers have adopted and written about more nuisance definitions. Oftentimes people who demonstrate moral courage are associated with nonconformist behaviors and research has primarily focused on the subject, suggesting that moral courage is "widely seen as an individualistic phenomenon driven by conscience" (Press 2018, 182). In general, definitions of moral courage contain a willingness to act, a disregard for the risks associated with the actions, and high sense of morality. The narrative that moral courage is an individual act is consistent with the current educational system in that it is framed by individual choice and singular acts. In the US educational system, where conformity and obedience to rules are rewarded and questioning and resistance are harshly admonished, moral courage becomes a threat to how success is achieved. Our understanding of moral courage is closely aligned with the civil rights, labor, and women's movement in the United States. In, "Courage in the Civil Rights Movement: A Resource for Educators," moral courage is defined as "speak[ing] through our inner conscious, guiding us to do the right thing despite the risks. It is choosing to put popularity and reputation aside to stand up for what we believe in" (https://www.civilrightsmuseum.org/educators). Per this resource, everyday people (like those involved in the US movement) develop everyday courage by practicing moral courage. In these examples, moral courage is a collective that is fueled by witnessing the consistent and constant acts of others while simultaneously developing one's own practice. Personally, we draw upon stories of moral courage from civil rights, women's, and labor movements that are steeped in community and interconnectedness. These stories made us question the stories that shaped both of our educational experiences.

Our relationship is an example of the power of storytelling. Caruthers reminds us that "a critical approach to storytelling challenges the ways knowledge is constructed, illuminates the relationship between knowledge and power, and redefines what is personal and political so that we learn to rewrite the dialectical connection between what we learn and how we come to define our history, experience, and language" (Caruthers 2006, 664). We connected through the stories we told about our work, our schooling experiences, and our experiences as faculty members and mothers. The more we told our individual stories, the stronger our connection became and it was as if we could really "see" the unique and authenticity of the other. Like all stories, embedded in our telling was our family's culture, history, and the values that shaped us. Also, embedded in those stories were our fears and anxieties about our professional positionalities and how our educational experiences feed those concerns. While different in many aspects, the stories we have in common forged the synergy that sparked more questions, ideas, and potential processes for creating change. Our storytelling process can be found in the literature, "The storytelling self is a social self, who declares and shapes important relationships through the mediating power of words" (Dyson & Genishi 1994, 5). Similarly, Leggo summarizes Hutchinson claims for the moral responsibilities of storytelling. She writes,

> Story is relational and reciprocal and, as such, entails moral responsibilities. As we tell stories and listen to stories, we stand in a moral relation to one another. The process itself is reciprocal, that is, I tell a

story and you listen, and then you tell a story and I listen. But the notion of reciprocity extends beyond this. Reciprocity does not simply mean that we share stories back and forth, but that we have an obligation to listen and tell in ways that will sustain the dignity of one another and avoid domination. (Leggo 2007, 93)

In this way, storytelling serves a function in uncovering and recovering our collective past so that we can reflect on them and reframe and regenerate options and advocacy for the future. Research suggests that integrated connectedness to a storytelling network has also been found to be the most important individual level factor in civic engagement that promotes collective efficacy and impact (Kim & Ball-Rokeach 2006). In sharing our stories, we acknowledged that most youth from our backgrounds do not "make it" despite their individual effort and hard work. The intersection of storytelling and advocacy, the location of stories that students like us did not hear in our schooling, is where we stand and ask educators about the stories that they tell about courage.

We entered this work centering stories because we believed that if we understood the stories that educators tell about courage then we could better prepare other educators to be courageous. We believed that if we better understood how individual stories about courageous advocacy intersect with the voices of their school community then we would learn how educators used their own identity and that of their students to better understand how inequity unfolded in their systems and structures. We believed that by hearing stories of courage then we would better understand the pathways toward collaborative story-making and civic engagement. Yet what you will read in this book is that courage, as a story, was less visible than the story of meritocracy in schools. Instead of stories about courage the data pointed toward the power of the meritocracy narrative of education in this country and compelled us to dissect our own educational stories to better understand how their telling framed our schooling experiences. In this first chapter we tell our individual stories. Gretchen, an African American woman born in the early 1970s and raised in the South in the 1970s and 1980s and Amy, a White woman born in the rust belt at the end of the 1970s and raised in the southwest in the 1980s and 1990s. In rendering our stories, we highlight how success and excellence as a product of hard work and perseverance is embedded in the fiber of our identities and we introduce how the power of the American Dream and the potency of the myth of meritocracy shapes our stories. We also share how family and school stories functioned in our lives to promote the perceived cause and effect relationships among the values of hard work, effort, and perseverance, and economic success in our minds and hearts through educational practices that focused on us as individuals and not the broken systems that we survived. After sharing our stories, we look back at them as a collection in an effort to better understand why sharing them with you is the first step to becoming aware of the salience of the meritocracy narrative in our individual stories across different time periods, cultures, and US contexts. We believe that looking at them as a collective, sets the stage for what the educators and students we interviewed face in schools today.

GRETCHEN'S NARRATIVE

> The pitcher cries for water to carry
> and a person for work that is real.
> (excerpt from "To Be of Use" from *Circles on the Water*, by Marge Piercy, 1982)

> De nigger woman is de mule uh de world so fur as Ah can see.
> (excerpt from *Their Eyes Were Watching God*, by Zora Neale Hurston, 1937)

Being the Bridge

My first memories of hearing stories take place on my maternal grandparents' front porch, and it was on the porch where I understood my connection to family and the multiple generations that raised me. The stories my family told have shaped my life immensely. These stories tell me who I am, where I come from, and what is expected of me. They are complicated stories. Some are stories of generosity and love, hard work and perseverance, while others are stories of regret and of people to fear. I was born to teenagers who married when they found out my mother was pregnant. When my father became physically abusive, she left. She was twenty years old with two children when she returned home to live with her parents. Two years later my father was shot and killed by the police. I was four years old when he was killed and it would be thirty-six years later before I knew the full story of his struggles with mental illness.

My family, like most, pick and choose the stories they pass on to the next generation. The majority of the stories I heard growing up centered on people who worked hard, overcame poverty and tragedy, supported family, and loved unconditionally. Generativity shapes most of the stories I recall, as evidenced by the reality that the people in my family's stories were primarily models of what and what not to be/do. The stories were told so that I would know the expectations for my own life. McAdams (2006) writes,

> Generativity is an adult's concern for or commitment to promoting the welfare and development of future generations. Generativity is the concern for or commitment to making the world better for the children

or other people's children, for the next generation, and for the generations to follow, going forward into the future. (xi)

Many of the stories are funny and when analyzed some are sad. Nevertheless, most were crafted for my well-being. This is the foundation of my family stories. The ones that I remember most are the ones told by the elder women in my life—my maternal grandmother and her sisters. They were the best storytellers!

As a small child, I can remember being with these women trying my best to imitate how they did things. Like most women of their generation, they told stories as they worked—snapping beans, canning fruits and vegetables, cleaning fish, shucking corn, or cleaning their elderly mother's house. At the core of these stories were their relationships with each other, their families, the community, and God. As an adult, I understand that the women in my life were not just telling stories as a means of communicating, they were theorizing (James, 1993). Connecting African storytelling traditions to philosophizing and theorizing James (1993) writes:

> Storytelling, theorizing in proverbs dedicated and responsive to the community, is essential for living thinkers. This is the medium of communication that binds the individual to the communal. It is perhaps the most effective means of instruction and theory. Maracle succinctly states the relationship: "There is a story in every line of theory [philosophy]. Philosophizing and theorizing in autobiographical storytelling are practices, in which we live our thoughts and recount our lives reflecting this." (35)

The stories that my grandmother and her sisters shared were filled with analysis and provided a window into their lives—lives that were not easy. After all, they were Black women born in rural Virginia in the early twentieth century. Their lives consisted of working on family farms and taking care of family. To achieve paid employment, they would have to leave their community. When they married young and started to have children, they stayed. They all married young and had children. Only one of them completed high school. They raised their children and struggled to make ends meet. When all of their children left home for college, they would work as cafeteria employees at nearby elementary schools. Important to note is that while their lives were shaped by racism, sexism, and poverty, they did not allow themselves to be shaped and defined by systems of oppression as demonstrated by their acts of love, generosity, and compassion. They were not mean and hardened women. In my world they were wise and beautiful, strong and all-knowing, hardworking and resilient. On the porch or in the garden, I felt safe in their presence. Reflecting back on that time, I have come to understand the immense benefit of growing up in an intergenerational household surrounded by strong, resilient women and being hugged by the stories they told. The foundation of how I understand myself is centered in that small rural community, what they modeled for me, and how their modeling shaped how I know the world.

Upon reflection, modeling was an act of love and my role models profoundly shaped my view of the world. Senge names these models, mental models. Mental models are the stories that we have playing in our head in observation of phenomenon. Senge argues these are deeply ingrained assumptions, generalizations, or even pictures or images that influence how we understand the world. When I imagine myself as an adult woman, images of myself as a worker are dominant and serve as lamp posts that light pathways for my decisions and actions. These mental models help me make sense of my context and my role in it. Senge states, "Mental models are active and they shape how we act" (Senge 1990, 175). Action is a critical aspect of Senge's definition of mental models. Likewise, action is critical to the formation of mental models. The women in my life were role models who demonstrated a way of being in the world that exuded purpose. They managed households, tended to people, and organized events. Most of their work was invisible to most of the world, yet they (and I) understood that what they did was integral to everyone's life.

When I began school, which they told me was my "work," I approached it with the same intentionality and purpose that was modeled for me. After all, I lived for the praise these women bestowed upon me, "She's a good worker, a really hard worker." Similarly, I always knew that I was the benefactor of the Civil Rights Movement, "ya'll don't know how hard we had it" was a statement I recall hearing repeatedly. Such words of encouragement bookmarked my entry into the hallways of formal education. My first schooling experience was in the rural community not far from my grandmother's front porch. Jefferson Elementary was a very special place. My storytelling aunts worked in the cafeteria and prepared real food such as rolls and cobblers, just like the food we had at home. And, like the food we had at home, we could get second helpings. Mrs. Key, my second-grade teacher, taught my aunts and uncles when they were in elementary school. She was also one of my storytellers, reminding me daily that she had students who were, "doctors and lawyers and that they lived in places all around the country."

It was during this time in my life that I recall my grandmother repeatedly saying to me, "You are old enough for your wants not to hurt you." It was usually said when I pronounced that I wanted something that I saw in a store or when I wanted to go somewhere. As a precocious seven-year-old, I understood this saying as having something to do with getting over (quickly) when I wanted something and did not get it. Reflecting back, it was a succinct statement of how the world would receive me. Ultimately, her saying would mean more to me when my mother moved us to the suburbs as she moved closer to work and us to a better school district.

We moved to the suburbs my third-grade year. Mom had lived at home for seven years, completing a college degree and saving money so that she could purchase a house for us. It was the first time that I would have my own room (with blue carpet that I picked out) and it was the first time that I would be a minority in the classroom. I remember these two things very distinctively. I loved my carpet and there was only one other Black kid in my classroom. I also remember that my storytellers were no longer with me daily. Fortunately for me, the seeds of my grandmother's stories had already been planted. While school was no longer an extension of my home life, I understood that I would go back home to Grandma's every weekend and that I would have to tell them how I was doing in school. In other words, my performance (achievement) in school had to remain the same. Failure was not an option. It was in this White schooling environment where the lessons I had been taught about hard work formally materialized. I observed my White peers intently. Becoming more fluent in White educational structures daily, I transferred the hard work of snapping, canning, shucking, and cleaning into the classroom and learning environment. In doing so, school success became a critical part of my identity and way of being in this White world despite the fact that school looked nothing like Grandma's front porch.

Bridging Grandma's front porch and my schooling was challenging. Things were so different in my new school and while my mother was an active parent, many of the things that I was experiencing were also new to her. It was not until becoming an adult and studying narrative that I truly understood how much a parent's narrative frames their offspring stories. It seems very obvious, but the immense depth of the connection was not apparent to me. As a child, I remember my mother's quiet demeanor and her inner resolve. She is the sixth child out of ten, a true middle child. Born into a large boisterous family, she is an observer, a pleaser, and, not surprisingly, a hard worker. All my life, I have felt the urge to protect her. I am sure it has much to do with the abuse she endured at the hands of my father. While I do not consciously remember it, it is clear to me that this infantile urge is embedded in my subconscious, my physiology, and my spirit. She left my father when she was twenty years old, with a three-month-old and nineteen-month-old. She went back home where she would endure the embarrassment of having to return and the weight of being abused. There were no counseling services; she was forced to make do. Fortunately for her and us, she had a place to go and while it was not perfect, it meant that she did not have to stay in a physically abusive marriage and she would not be homeless with two children. As a child, it was my understanding that her family saved us. Mom would rebound from her abuse as indicated by her completing college, getting a "good-paying job" at a fortune 500 company, and saving to buy a house where my brother and I could attend "good schools." Eventually, she would put us through college, we would graduate, and proceed to live our own lives.

Her story reads like the redemptive narratives outlined in McAdams work, *The Redemptive Self: Stories Americans Live By*. He writes,

> In their personal battles against a wide range of opponents, the African American adults in our sample mobilized resources and marshaled forces of many different kinds. Although they had opponents, they also had many allies. The traditional European American emphasis on rugged individualism seems tempered in these stories. The protagonists often enjoy considerable support from a community of family, friends, and institutions that are allied with them against the opponents of life. (McAdams 2006, 177)

Mom's stories center other people and that she had a support system that provided a safe place for her to return. She often told stories about the people who assisted and helped her. Yet, she was reluctant to tell stories about herself. To this day, I have to poke and prod to get her to tell her story. In doing so, I have learned so much about who my mother is and a glimpse into some of the reasons why she does not share or even think of her story as one that warrants sharing. For example, it was not until I was in graduate school writing about integration in North Carolina that I learned that she had, in fact, integrated her own high school. The stories of her being bullied are filled with holes that I imagined are intentionally blocked out. It's how she has managed to thrive after enduring so much. When I ask her why she attends the high school reunions with people who were so mean to her she responds, "I go back to let them know that I am doing well. Hey, I did just as well as they did. You know, I am not going to let their prejudices define me." To this day, my mother credits her children's success to our own hard work and her intentional prayers, "I always prayed that whatever blessings that God had in store for me that they be bestowed upon my children." Her selflessness is central to her sense of self and it is how I continue to experience her as her adult child. This amazing strength is also her weakness. As a young child and young adult, one of the ways that I worked to make my mother's strength known and visible to others was to achieve. In my young, impressionable mind, my success would be hers.

BUILDING THE BRIDGE

"Beginning in our teenage years, we endeavor to understand our lives as grand narratives, reconstructing the past and imagining the future in such a way as to provide our lives with some semblance of purpose, unity, and meaning. Our stories provide justification and motivation for the lives we have chosen to lead" (McAdams 2006, xiii).

o sing to me a song of hope
that gives me ways
to walk a path

o sing to me a song of hope
that leads me home
that leads me home
—Excerpt from "untitled," by emt

I have reflected a lot about how my lived experiences shape my understanding of my role as a learner. My friend Mark Hicks and I wrote about our teenage selves and how those identities shape our work in cross-cultural communities. We wrote;

> Part of our struggle was the internalized belief that we could "be everything to everybody," that choosing one group over another would somehow exclude yourself from that community. This, to our mind, was not acceptable for "being included" was the essence of the game. (Hicks & Generett 2011, 688)

For Black kids in integrated schools, the games were dynamic, multifaceted, and complex. Something as simple as a birthday party in the 1980s posed a dilemma as to which friends you invited to the party (honors class White friends or my neighborhood Black friends). I had not yet figured out how to bridge the two. I had also not been introduced to theories on racial identity development. When I did read about them, the theories seemed blatantly obvious to me.

My mother's response to my schooling experience was like her response to most things, tempered. As long as I did my best, she was fine with the results. A's and the occasional C garnered the same response, "Is this your best?" The one time I got a C on my report card was in the fourth grade and it was in conduct. I did not make the honor roll because of that C and Mom was puzzled because misbehaving was not an option for my brother and me. When my teacher said that I got a C because I was too "eager," often raising my hand too loudly or sharing the answer with others, Mom was not phased. She came home and told me that it was okay to get C's in conduct in the fourth grade. I never heard another word about it. She supported whatever I wanted to do—sports, homecoming court, talent shows, student government, whatever. I did everything in school because I could and I did so without asking why or to what ends. My school choices imitated the models of success presented to me. All of my mother's sisters and brothers were active in their schools and had all gone to college and beyond. My father's siblings also expected us to go to college. In school, I would be a model of academic success and good behavior. My parent's poor upbringing, commitment to hard work, and dedication to persevering left little doubt about the expectations for my own life. Whether by family modeling or the expectation of assimilation forced by my school's Western European curriculum, I internalized what Ibram X. Kendi names, "uplift suasion." He writes that, "uplift suasion was based on the idea that White people could be persuaded away from their racist ideas if they saw Black people improving their behavior, uplifting themselves from low station in American society" (124). The burden of race relations was placed squarely on the shoulders of Black Americans. "Positive Black behavior, abolitionist strategist held, undermined racist ideas, and negative Black behavior confirmed them" (124). Kendi's definition is used in reference to eighteenth-century US history, yet highlights how such racist ideas continue to be central in our current context.

My response to being the only Black student in a classroom or in a program was to work harder, be friendlier, and learn the cultural norms of everyone in the room. By the twelfth grade, I was exhausted and decided that I would not do this anymore. Without having the words, my spirit felt the weight of what it meant to be in all White spaces without a framing of what it was or how to respond to it with a critical eye. Kendi writes that uplift suasion is flawed because it is racist. First, it assumes that "racist ideas were sensible and could be undone by appealing to sensibilities" (Kendi 2017, 125). Second, that "uplift suasion also failed to account for the widespread belief in the extraordinary Negro, which had dominated assimilationist and abolitionist thinking in America for a century. Upwardly mobile Blacks were regularly cast aside as unique and as different from ordinary, inferior Black people" (Kendi 2017, 125). Always being the "chosen" Black kid made me question, "Why me and not others that looked like me?" I knew that my Black friends were just as capable. As I matriculated through high school, I began to question the view that assimilating into White spaces was normal and necessary in order to achieve success and excellence. I had lots of questions that I did not have the words to ask and it was clear to me that my participation in these spaces made me feel less and less as if I mattered. I sought out a different way of being in the world.

I decided to attend Spelman College, a historically Black women's college. My eighteen-year-old self was filled with excitement and anticipation at my first convocation meeting. Convocation were mandatory gatherings in Sister's Chapel where the entire first year class gathered for a non-denominational service designed to pass on traditions from one class to the next. Dr. Johnnetta Cole, our Sister President (as we called her), began the gathering by telling us to, "look left and now look right." Traditionally, the saying goes, "because one of you will not be here by the end of the year or at graduation." Yet, our Sister President said something different and it forever changed how I thought about schooling and learning. She said, "If all of you are not here at graduation, we have failed." Knowing that I was not alone and that others were committed to my success felt like being on Grandma's porch snapping beans.

WALKING THE BRIDGE

I am not sure what I did that made me jump from the porch and run toward Ma Maggie's house. I just knew that I was in trouble and that Grandma was not going to chase after me. I stopped when I was far away as not to be caught, but still within earshot. Grandma stood on the porch in her housecoat with her hands on her hips and yelled out to me, "You have to come back."

> you
> opened
> the
> door
>   and
>   we
>   have
>   entered.
> —by Gloria Wade-Gayles from *Anointed to Fly*

My first year at Spelman College was the first time I experienced Black women's lived experiences at the center of my education including curriculum, leadership, and all things social. I was often amazed at the pure delight and pleasure that I took in being with my peers as I witnessed their genius and tenacity. It was the first time since Jefferson Elementary that I had Black teachers. The familiar ways of being in classrooms where learning was communal and stories were as central as the text was the norm. I learned from women like Johnnetta Cole, Beverly Guy-Sheftall, and Ruth Simmons. Perhaps most importantly, there was nothing "special" about me. There were smart Black women all around. It was wonderful to know that I was not alone, "If the Civil Rights Movement is 'dead,' and if it gave us nothing else, it gave us each other forever" (Alice Walker quoted in Hendrickson 1999, 111). And, in giving us to each other, it was clear that we were being prepared to create spaces for others like us.

I began to reimagine the saying, "To whom much is given, much is expected." The fact that I had been given this opportunity meant that I had to do something with it and my something would be to model after the Black women leaders and professors that I was privileged to encounter, like I had originally modeled after my grandmother, great-aunts, and mother. Having the benefit of being fluent in White spaces, I would work to create more opportunities for students like me (and them) all while demonstrating that all we needed was access and opportunity to show our capabilities. I would use what I learned at Spelman and be like the women I met there.

I first learned about intersectionality in a women's studies class taught by Beverly Guy-Sheftall. Today, Collins and Bilge define intersectionality as;

> a way of understanding and analyzing the complexity of the world, in people, and in human experiences. The events and conditions of social and political life and the self can seldom be understood as shaped by one factor. They are generally shaped by many factors in diverse and mutually influencing ways. When it comes to social inequality, people's lives and the organization of power in a given society are social division, be it race or gender or class, but many axes that work together and influence each other. Intersectionality as an analytical tool gives people better access to the complexity of the world and of themselves. (Collins & Bilge 2016, 2)

It was the first time that I vividly recalled having the words to name my experiences and realized that, through narratives, tools could be designed to transform how people think. In my naivete, I imagined myself bringing forth this information and more like it to people eager to act differently and make different (less oppressive) decisions. I was, as I later wrote, "audaciously hopeful" (Hicks & Generett 2011). Meaning, I was hopeful in the belief that Black people, like me, would be seen and included equally within structures (the notion of progress) even when there was little evidence to suggest that our effort would produce a positive effect (Generett & Hicks 2004). I decided to go to graduate school.

For this reason, I decided to attend graduate school. I matriculated into the University of North Carolina at Chapel Hill and transitioning back into a White-centered learning environment was difficult for me. The progressive mindsets of many of my White peers had been achieved in theory and in their scholarship, but not through the deep interrogation of their personal narratives. Working to create a research agenda, I found myself struggling to walk the bridge in this space. The marginalization I experienced at the beginning of my graduate school experience was palatable. My classes were back to what I had experienced in high school, me being the exception and Whiteness (including every picture on every wall) looking down upon us all. Intersectionality had never been so real as that first year. I am eternally grateful to my intellectual role models in educational research such as Jackie Jordan Irvine, Vanessa Siddle-Walker, Michele Foster, Patricia Hill-Collins, Lisa Delpit, Gloria Ladson-Billings, and bell hooks whose academic work built on the foundational work I started in college. Using the work of these women, I forged a career in education with the goals of adding to their work, of being the next generation to capture Black American narratives, and to better train educators to work with Black students.

Over the past twenty years, I have served on the faculty of four institutions. Not much has changed from my graduate school experience where Whiteness looks down upon everything. Despite the fact that I have moved up the ranks to a full professor and have served in numerous administrative roles, I still find what my colleague Sheryl Conrad Cozart and I wrote "Intellectually, we are well prepared; however, something is missing" (Generett & Cozart 2011, 147).

I have worked hard to walk the bridge, to allow my narrative and the stories that shaped me to influence my decisions and actions on behalf of those historically underserved, under-resourced, and underrepresented students and peers. This has been difficult work as evidenced by the limited numbers of Black professors at every rank. Given that the production of scholarship is central to sustaining the inequities in the academy any "Scholarship by and about [non-White] people . . . is viewed as a dangerous tainting of educational quality" (Farmer 1993, 197). As the only Black woman in every department that I have served in at the four predominantly White institutions (PWI), where I have worked I have a theoretical and practical understanding of this experience. At times I am paralyzed by my inability to create change. Specifically, there are days when my inability to connect the work of the academy—teaching, service, and research—to my commitment to serving my community is heartbreaking. So, I walk the bridge. I go back to the porch and my college classes where I recall the stories that I heard and use them as the theoretical bridging that ties together all of who I am in the academy together.

So, who am I in the academy and what do I do? My research and teaching are designed to bridge the gap between scholarship and practice by focusing on the development of socially just educators and educational leaders. I am a qualitative researcher who tells stories about education in America. My research started with my own narrative as a young girl schooled in suburban Richmond, yet tethered to my grandmother's front porch in rural Virginia. Blending the arts and sciences in my methodology, I use stories to capture the complex, dynamic, and multifaceted ways in which race, class, and gender shape our relationships to schooling. Storytelling, in its simplest form, is a way of relating to and informing one another. As a researcher, I have come to understand that there is a deeper benefit; telling stories offers a place where we can reflect and recast our individual stories to form a collective narrative that can be used as a catalyst for our own personal growth and community development. Similarly, our collective, reimagined stories can be used to create more equitable and just schools and organizations. Ultimately, reflective and interactive storytelling serves a function in uncovering and recovering our individual and collective stories so that we can disrupt systemic inequities.

As a teacher, I have worked very hard to develop my pedagogical stance. While expertise and knowledge drives what I teach, how I teach is what makes a difference in my students' learning. I believe that teaching is relational. I also believe that excellent teaching requires that you make a commitment, not just to content expertise, but to designing curriculum that meets adult learners where they are while providing a clear process for where you ultimately want student learning to go. In addition to critical self-reflection, this pedagogical stance requires that I am committed to designing courses so that students see themselves as an integral part of the content and that the processes I design are accessible to them. I believe that students must envision their current and future selves in the content in order to "hold on to it" with the final goal being that students use the presented information in ways that make their communities more equitable and just.

This work is very important to me and it is exhausting. Like the redemption narratives constructed by successful people, I was brought up in an educational system that told me that what I do is more important than who I am. And, like the Black women at Spelman College who modeled for me, I would model for others the possibilities offered at the intersections. In other words, I would claim my space and work to bring my whole self into the academy. So, it is no wonder that my recollections of schooling experiences and ways of being in the world connect me to models of productivity (home life) and professionalism (Spelman experience). Inherently racist and sexist systems place value on productivity and if I, as a professor in the academy, am to increase access and opportunity for my communities then I must meet the productivity demands placed upon me as the cost for improving the possibilities for my communities (Cook & Generett 2019, 131).

One of my most powerful memories at Spelman came in Dr. Gloria Wade-Gayles's English class; Dr. Wade-Gayles is an amazing teacher and a force with words. On this particular day, we were discussing *Beloved*, by Pulitzer Prize winner Toni Morrison and during the discussion she told the class to, "claim your space." She went on to explain that we had every right to the space we occupied on the earth, but that no one was going to allow us to be in that space, that we would have to "claim it." At the time, I was not sure what Dr. Wade-Gayles actually meant by saying those three words. Over twenty-five years later, they mean so much. Claim your space means to put a stake down and to not allow others to render me invisible. Claim your space are three words that remind me that I am worthy and that what I contribute to the academy makes it better able to serve all students.

I have found my purpose in the academy, for now. Within the stories of hard work and perseverance, it can be difficult to understand who you existentially are and how to hold on to your stories and at the same time, not be shackled by them. Walking the bridge has become a type of spiritual process for me. Grandma and my great-aunts are no longer physically with me, but I feel their presence when I am at leadership tables and people attempt to make decisions that devalue people like them and like me. I plant my feet solidly on the floor and claim my space and in doing so, I imagine that they are there supporting me. Some Black academics have written similar stances as a critical part of how they enact their spirituality in the academy. Cynthia Dillard (2002) writes, "The more stories we 'uncover' from multiple cultural spaces, the more able we might be to foster a balance of the spiritual, emotional, and intellectual development of ourselves and our students in today's culturally diverse settings" (p. 386).

On August 5, 2019, Toni Morrison transitioned. Her loss is palatable and her gifts, immeasurable. I used the day to reflect on the impact of her work on my life and then on August 8, the *Guardian* published one of her essays from *Mouth Full of Blood: Essays, Speeches, Mediations*. In an essay from her personal archives she writes:

> Mindful of and rebellious towards the cultural and racial expectations and impositions my fiction would encourage, it was important for me not to reveal, that is, reinforce, already established reality (literary or historical) that the reader and I agree upon beforehand. I could not, without engaging in another kind of cultural totalising process, assume or exercise that kind of authority. It was in *Beloved* that all of these matters coalesced for me in new and major ways. History versus memory, and memory versus memorylessness. Rememory as in recollecting and remembering as in reassembling the members of the body, the family, the population of the past. And it was the struggle, the pitched battle between remembering and forgetting, that became the device of the narrative. The effort to both remember and not know became the structure of the text. (https://www.theguardian.com/books/2019/aug/08/toni-morrison-rememory-essay)

Toni Morrison's work reminds me of the simultaneous importance of remembering the stories that shaped me and not allowing them to limit my understanding of the possibilities for the future. Having done the work of integrating my own narrative, I am more aware of the unchallenged assumptions that I bring into any space and I am conscious of how these assumptions shape my expectations of my colleagues and the academy. Similarly, I am more aware of how my own lived history and the good intentions that shape the telling of these stories in my life inform my beliefs and values. For example, as a benefactor of the US Civil Rights Movement, I am aware of how that narrative is subject to repetition, much like the narrative of the American Dream. By being aware of this narrative, remembering it, I have the power to transform it.

AMY'S NARRATIVE

Every Good Girl Does Well

Family stories have shaped my storytelling. I fold my stories into the familiar outlines. I tell them to my boys. My boys fold themselves in as well. It is our story.

Our family stories came from our lives just as much as they were brought into our homes in hardcovers and paperbacks. It is somehow easier to set the stage with the stories that were brought in.

I read Horatio Alger Jr.'s stories growing up. My great-grandmother on my father's side had collected a nearly full set when she was growing up. She parceled them out to her children who then parceled them out to their children. My lot was seven novels that sat on the shelf of the old entertainment center my dad built and my mom stained, above the old TV and across from the turntable. I read and re-read them, careful with the crumbling corners of their pages. My favorite was the 1905 novel, *Tom the Bootblack: Or the Road to Success.* Alger taught me the simplest stories. Every good boy (i.e., every good boy with a strong worth ethic who does his job honestly and without complaint) does well. The books were always about boys, but the tooth fairy had left me a Susan B. Anthony dollar coin and a note encouraging me to read about women's suffrage and I knew at the age of seven that I lived in a time when every good girl could do as well as every good boy.

I had my own set of novels too, gifted to me by an uncle for my eighth birthday. They were the Laura Ingalls Wilder *Little House on the Prairie* books. Finally, a narrative in which every good girl does well! The novels exhaustively detail the hard work of women's everyday lives, and how it is your responsibility to both do the work and find the fun in it. Maybe I loved them in that they sounded like the stories of my grandmothers (e.g., games played with shelled peas, boiled eggs, or jars of jam and pickles after the hard work of shelling, boiling, and canning). Both my grandmothers had spent their childhoods on farms before the city's industrial center pulled them in.

I read and reread these simple stories about how to work hard and succeed. But the truth is stories are complicated. The hero(ine) does not win every battle, even if she wins the war. Despite a willingness to work hard, the obstacles may (occasionally) form into hills too big and too many for us to climb. Another lesson I had learned was to really think about whether this is the hill I wanted to die on.

I do not remember the house on Donovan Street. I have been told I became a big sister there and I have seen the pictures of me holding my doll (Baby David) as my mom held my brother (Baby Josh, still pronounced Dosh in my heart). I was a big sister and my brother was Baby Dosh, who became Boy Cub (after I saw *The Jungle Book*), who became

Kid Boy (after we read Samuel Delaney's *Star Pit*), who became KB because we were both too old and too cool to explain, who finally became a mystery to me.

I was a big sister and a good girl who would do well, but my stories began in the dry desert air, rows of little houses with wheels, each about the same size and shape as its neighbors but decorated with plants or signs or wooden animals to show how its family was different from all those around them.

I was born to the great American Love Story. My mom was a cheerleader and my dad was a football player. Their families went to the same churches and schools. They started dating at fifteen, married at twenty, and had me at twenty-two. They had brothers and sisters, aunts and uncles, cousins and second cousins, parents and grandparents all around them. But they left, taking just me and my brother, to move across the country, to find work, to live a better life, to get the American Dream. It was just the four of us in a trailer two thousand miles away from family and maybe I felt a bit like I was Laura living with her Ma and Pa and sister in *The Little House in the Big Woods*. I was a big sister, I could work hard, and I would do well.

As a White family in the 1980s, we were privileged enough to believe in colorblindness and equality and not yet aware enough of the structures and systems that supported us. When I worried about discrimination or prejudice, it was because, yet another woman grabbed up her purse from the grocery cart as my dad with his long hair and work rough hands walked by. I felt safe with those hands, but she did not.

My folks worked hard, and we moved up and out, eventually settling in a working-class suburb with good schools where I could work hard and would do well. If school was to be my work, then I would work hard, honestly, and without complaint—just like Tom and Laura, just like my grandmothers, just like my mom and dad. I held my pencil just right (efficiently up and down so you wear it down evenly and do not have to go to the pencil sharpener as often), wrote neatly, read everything put in front of me, did all the homework, and I knew all the answers if the teacher called on me (but I never would brag that I knew them by raising my hand). I was visible only in that I was so invisible; I never drew bad attention.

School was my job, and like my grandmothers and mother, I still had a second shift (Hochschild 1989). I was a big sister, and we were latchkey kids. We walked home from school, made snacks, did our homework, and completed the assigned chores posted to the calendar on the fridge. Like my grandmothers and mother, we made games of dusting, vacuuming, sweeping, mopping, washing dishes, and cleaning toilets. Yet I did not know the extent to which I had taken up their modeling until the day when KB rolled his eyes and wished we had a genie or a robot, something, *anything*, to do our boring, *old* chores for us. Out of my mouth came my grandmothers' "If wishes were horses, beggars would ride," mimicked with all the nose-wrinkled derision a child could muster. I had already learned there was something amoral about depending on others. Hard work is its own reward, but the only work worth anything is work you do with your own two hands.

Nose to the Grindstone

It was not until seventh grade that I thought much about learning as anything beyond the work you do with your own two hands in school. That year, school changed for me due to a girl, more acquaintance than friend. Later, I learned that her parents were immigrants and believers in the American Dream. They wanted the best for their daughter and believed education opened doors. They enrolled her in advanced courses (mathematics since the United States was just becoming focused on the power of a STEM education) at the community college and now she was ready for algebra. We were in seventh grade, but they only taught algebra to eighth graders (and even then, the teacher cited Piaget's formal operational stage as a reason that she believed children *like us* should not be exposed to algebra until high school). The girl was afraid to go alone and suddenly my invisibility disappeared. All I knew about the backstory was that I would be accompanying her to math classes with the eighth graders.

I confided in a favorite teacher that I was nervous and unprepared, math was my worst subject and I had not taken the preliminary coursework. I was told not to worry, "Failure might be good for you, and anyway, it never hurts to keep your nose to the grindstone." Three months in and I felt like I was treading water. I was exhaustively staying afloat, but I was not getting ahead. Having always been at the "head of the class," this was the first time I realized school was competition. Hard work was *not* its own reward. Hard work was to get ahead. I persevered.

Six months in, the other girl had failed out and was back in seventh grade (A real tragedy—she later went onto an Ivy League and died by suicide in her freshman dorm. We only knew each other in passing by then, but I wondered how I had missed the signs in seventh grade). The school had a problem they had not prepared for now. What to do with me? As we headed into the home stretch of the school year, I had already taken and passed the highest math course they offered. It was decided to test me for a gifted program they were opening at the high school. If I passed, I could go onto ninth grade the following year. Problem solved. If not, additional thought would need to be put into the plans. I was presented with the "opportunity" and seriously considered purposefully failing the test. I did not want to go to high school. I wished to go back to seventh grade with my friends. But if wishes were horses, beggars would ride. And to do less than my best was dishonest. To do anything less than your best is to sacrifice the gift (so said Steve Prefontaine). Needless to say, I passed.

Don't Let Them Out Work You

I lost my brother when I was twenty-nine. I had a young son and was pregnant with my second. KB, who had issues with his health, migraines, and opioid addiction, was staying with my folks when I called home to tell my mom the latest stories of her grandsons. He did not want to speak with me, but my mom cajoled him, phone held out so I could hear both sides of their argument. He picked up the phone and we had a conversation like strangers. I was too polite and wrapped in my niceness. I don't know what it was like on his side. It was the last time I spoke with him. He left their home later that week, they heard from him a few times in the following month, and then he was gone. My parents protected me, hiding his stories under their own. Each hint of a story, mentioned in passing over a dozen years, raises a new possibility. He left with a gun and a threat that he would kill himself. He left with a truck and a desire for peace in the desert. He left for a girl that he lost or maybe that he hoped to win. He left and was never heard from again. I will never be able to piece together his narrative. I fear I will never stop trying.

The thing is—where I was smart, KB was brilliant. Where I worked hard, he was effortless. I faked it where he made it. He was always visible under the spotlight. And I think that maybe school was not good to him. Maybe schools want the quiet kids who hold their pencils just right and are always afraid that they are not working hard enough, that someone else will outwork them.

But that is not the story I want us to tell. Telling my story makes me aware of the outlines of the stories I have grown up within. I want to push and pull and transform the edges. I want us to work hard, but also to not be afraid that others will out work us. I want us to recognize community over competition. But to be honest, I don't know how.

Stories as Windows into What's Possible and What's Not Possible

The stories we were told in our families, the stories that our teachers told us, and how we took up those stories suggest that in telling the dominant narrative of meritocracy, we miss the opportunity to tell a different story, a story of community and collaboration. Gretchen's schooling was defined by a life in constant motion and navigation, working to bridge the gap between home, school, and community. Amy's school experience was framed through stories about the honesty of hard work and immorality of doing less than your best; she learned to show up and to never stop working. There were places where the stories told to us by our families, the ones that grounded us the most were the very ones that marginalized us in school. So, we learned to keep them to ourselves. Reflecting back on these experiences we cannot help to imagine how the outcomes for students like us might be different if the stories shared in schools focused less on individualism and more on community. What if community stories were a critical part of the stories we tell in schools and about the value of education? Caruthers (2006) offers three key concepts that support the use of stories—voice, inquiry, and knowledge. Uplifting voices, when doing community engagement work, allows us to connect and make use of collective meaning. Britzman (1990) pointed out that voice implies "the individual's relationship to the meaning of her/his experience and hence, to language, and the individual's relationship to the other." People should challenge systemic issues, that are typically seen as normative, by learning to inquire/question their individual and personal experiences. "Inquiry is necessary at the outset for forming personal purpose. While the latter comes from within, it must be fueled by information, ideas, dilemmas, and other contentions in our environment" (Fullan 1993, 15). We can help others question their experiences and acquire personal knowledge when it comes to combating and addressing difficult topics such as race/ethnicity, class, and gender. Doing so would encourage social transformation and reimaging what school systems and the people in those systems look like.

In the chapters that follow, we interrogate the stories that teachers tell, how their students understand them or "pick them up," and end with cases designed to imagine all of us telling different types of stories about educational success. In doing so, we channel the words of Maxine Greene. She writes, "imagination, as is well known, is the capacity that enables us to move through the barriers of the taken-for-granted and summon up alternative possibilities for living, for being in the world. It permits us to set aside (at least for a while) the stiflingly familiar and the banal. It opens us to visions of the possible rather than the predictable; it permits us, if we choose to give our imaginations free play, to look at things as if they could be otherwise" (Greene 1995, 494). As you go through this text, we ask that you consider how our stories read together and with the stories of the educators and students in this book. We ask that you consider how the stories we tell about success in schools force students to bear the weight of educational inequities as opposed to transforming the system to better serve youth and their families. In the end, we ask that you look at things as if they could be otherwise.

TWO

The Stories Educators Tell

In this chapter, we tell the stories of our culture writ large as well as the stories shared with us by teachers. We begin with the US meritocratic master narrative, a myth that individual stories seem to reinscribe, even when they are not aware or do not intend to do so. We should note this is not the story we intended to (re)tell. We sought out and intended to tell educators' stories of moral courage, grounded in self-sacrifice for the good of their students. We expected to tell stories of educators standing up, speaking out, and being willing to confront social disapproval and disappointment in the service of their students and the larger communities in which their schools are situated. We envisioned the kind of storytelling that is synonymous with the civic and social movements that are writ large in our own memories—civil rights, women's rights, and labor movements. We hoped to uncover courageous stories that would pour into readers, give hope, and act to sustain the efforts of educators and educational leaders working to right inequitable systems. We believed that if we shared the stories that educators tell about courage, that we could better prepare current and future educators to be courageous and take up the fight for equitable education for all students.

Nonetheless, we begin with the "American Dream" because both the stories shared with us and our own stories (see chapter 1) unintentionally center a uniquely American merit narrative that affirms opportunity to all who work hard. We did not expect to start here, but we cannot deny there is something seductive and pernicious about fitting one's individual story into the larger cultural framework. We hope that by sharing the stories that necessitated a shift in lens from courage to merit, we can begin to lay the groundwork for pushing the boundaries of a meritocratic style of storytelling that has traditionally distinguished America from other countries in the world. We begin by arguing that while American literature, popular media, federal, state, and local policy reify the idealism of the American Dream, it is within our educational system that this work highlights the power and continued impact of the narrative on today's youth.

Next, we present the journey line protocol as a qualitative methodology that centers personal stories and narratives as critical to how we make meaning of the world and ourselves. As used here, the journey line methodology provides insight into how educators understand success and courage, opportunity and access, and their own identities as advocates for equity. Six educators, four classroom teachers and two social workers, are introduced as having completed journey lines where they were specifically asked about courage in the profession. The resulting themes—hard work and perseverance, support of talent, advocacy and navigation, protection of students, support of colleagues, and going beyond expectations—may not have fit within the bounds of our preconceived notions about moral courage, but each theme is deeply connected to how the educators understand their stories as preparing their students for success after high school. We discuss both the overwhelming prevalence of these meritocratic themes (hard work, perseverance, support of individual talent, and going beyond expectations) and our concerns for the limitations of these framings for critical analyses of inequities, community advocacy, and navigation of existing systems.

US MERITOCRACY: WHAT IS A MASTER NARRATIVE?

In the United States, meritocracy is a master narrative that profoundly affects Americans' understanding of what it means to be successful contributors to society. In describing master narratives, Mishler writes,

> Master narratives define rights and duties and incorporate the values of the dominant social and political groups. Their unexamined taken-for-granted assumptions about how the world is and ought to be conceal patterns of domination and submission. Like all narratives, these are selective representations excluding experiences and views of some sectors of society while including and privileging others. (Mishler 1995, 114)

Mishler's description makes clear how master narratives describe an individual's contribution to society from the perspective of dominant members of that society, such that they function to maintain the status quo of social hierarchies through the application of unexamined assumptions for why these hierarchies exist.

We further argue that master narratives define what it means to be successful in culturally relevant ways. In particular, the master narrative tends to reify existing gender, race, and class power imbalances because it assumes that the current state of society (i.e., the privilege of some, such as White men, to access opportunities through which they may gain success) is normative and consistent with cultural values. The recognition of race, gender, and class power imbalances becomes subsumed to the cultural master narrative as the underlying assumptions of what it takes to be successful are spotlighted.

Moreover, master narratives have staying power. Halverson, Goodall, and Corman (2011) distinguish master narratives from individual stories due to their incredible resilience over long periods of time, during which they become deeply embedded in culture and in fact serve to define the status quo. In this way, master narratives become generally known or shared by all members of a culture. Thus, even when we sought out stories about courage in the face of normative and inequitable structures, we told and were told stories that reinscribed elements of the American master narrative.

Meaning Making: The Translation of the Master Narrative to an Individual's Journey Line

Asking for courage and receiving meritocracy occurs because, being normative, master narratives are internalized and reproduced by individuals within a culture (Sandlin & Clark 2009). Thus, individuals may tell stories of their own life that illustrate elements of the master narrative. In particular, Americans may tell stories that lift up their own success as illustrative of meritocratic values. Individuals further make overall sense of the collection of their personal stories as a personal narrative (i.e., journey line) that reproduces the framing of the cultural master narrative. Put simply, each success story reifies elements of the American meritocratic myth, while the overall life journey is seen as a series of successes and obstacles overcome on the way to obtaining success.

Another way in which the meritocratic master narrative is retold by Americans is through the tendency to take on a "redemptive self" narrative as they tell their own stories and make sense of their individual journeys. McAdams (2006) offers the typical American plot outline of this "redemptive self" narrative. He argues that Americans first come to see themselves as having a special talent, advantage, or gift (i.e., merit) that seemingly sets them apart from others. This awareness makes us acutely aware of the difficulties others face because they lack the same merits. He suggests that recognition of a talent makes us simultaneously feel special and guilty. The positive recognition inspires a sense of responsibility (and guilt that we might be shirking it) and we are motivated to put our gifts in the service of others. The pervasiveness of this message is significant. For example, quite recently, this ideal was captured again in the superhero franchises that reiterate that with great power, talents, or gifts, comes great responsibility.

As with any good story, despite our merit, we encounter many obstacles to both our personal and interpersonal goals along the way. These obstacles are either overcome due to our hard work and perseverance in pursuit of our special talents and responsibilities or they result in failures, that at least have the benefit of teaching us important life lessons. At the heart of this common and repeated story, McAdams (2006) suggests that Americans feel torn between the self-reinforcing nature of their own success and guilt and responsibility about putting their efforts and talents in service of their communities. A successful, healthy resolution of this conflict is a generative focus, in which the successful leave behind a positive individual legacy due to their efforts and contributions to the community, next generation, and so forth.

Moreover, the ways that our personal stories are pulled together to form identity narratives are central to the ways we function and enact our practice. As Lakoff and Johnson explain,

> The concepts that govern our thoughts are not just matters of the intellect. They also govern our everyday functioning, down to the most mundane details. Our concepts structure what we perceive, how we get around in the world, and how we relate to other people. Our conceptual system thus plays a central role in defining our everyday realities. If we are right in suggesting that our conceptual system is largely metaphorical, then the way we think, what we experience and what we do every day is very much a matter of metaphor. (2003, 3)

Put simply, meritocracy is deeply embedded in the ways that Americans think about and share stories of their successes. The stories we shared in chapter 1 take up elements of meritocracy because we enact cultural metaphors in our everyday practice. We see and celebrate our own hard work and perseverance in understanding our success, and as we will show in this chapter and the next, we are not alone. Further, we argue that it is difficult to break out of the master narrative framing to tell different stories, even when we want to.

The American Dream as a Master Narrative of Meritocracy

So, what is meritocracy? As a master narrative, the tenets of meritocracy are broadly defined as the beliefs that those who are successful have earned it through hard work, perseverance, and application of individual talent. Thus, those who benefit in a meritocratic system "believe they have earned whatever rewards they have come to possess" (Liu 2011, 386). Importantly, the American meritocratic myth does not define what constitutes merit. The abstractness of this central idea means that the master narrative operates insidiously. Individuals must rely on their unique contexts to determine what is worthy of merit, but to the extent that they see themselves as successful, their stories will reflect having earned that success through hard work, perseverance, and application of their talents in service of self and others.

The American Dream is the most obvious way in which the myth of meritocracy is embedded in the very fabric of US culture. At its heart, the American Dream advances the idea that those who are successful have "earned" their success through identifying their individual strengths, talents, or opportunities and applying these to advance themselves individually. However, demonstration of merit requires hard work. There is an expectation that it is not easy for anyone, no matter how privileged. In the United States, the cultural "truth" is that we all must "pull ourselves up by our bootstraps." It is expected that challenges will arise, including both temporary and catastrophic setbacks. The successful individual perseveres over such challenges, rising up over peers and redeeming failures.

The primary tenet of hard work and perseverance lies at the heart of the meritocratic master narrative in the United States. In particular, the central focus on hard work arose historically with the influx of Protestant (Puritan) colonizers (Young 2011). Weber (1958) famously tied these values to the tenets of US capitalism, and as seen in the next section, to the shift from class mobility to economic prosperity. Today, hard work remains a central component of American psyche, with 86 percent of Democrats and 91 percent of Republicans believing that a strong work ethic is the single strongest contributor to attaining the American Dream (GALEWiLL Center 2012).

A second tenet of the American meritocratic master narrative is hyper-individualism. Individualism, a belief that people are different from others and have rights to autonomy and independence such that their own interests prevail over the collective interest (Loose 2008), is a dominant feature in Western culture (Riesman 1961). In the United States, individualism is taken to an extreme in which the very foundation of American identity, the US Constitution, frames foundational rights in terms of the individual rather than the collective. As a tenet of the master narrative, individual focus on hard work and perseverance serve to minimize the extent to which context, and in particular systemic and structural constraints, serve to limit access to opportunities for success.

The American Dream, Class Mobility, and Economic Prosperity

The initial concept of the American Dream is credited to Alexis de Tocqueville, a French diplomat, political theorist, and sociologist who traveled around the United States in the early 1830s. He initially came to the United States to study the prison system, but his record of observations about "uniquely American" cultural values were collected in 1835 in *Democracy in America*.

On one hand, de Tocqueville was complimentary of American culture and politics, arguing that the US democratic system offered the most advanced example of individual equality in the world. The "American Dream" was a term he coined to describe "the charm of anticipated success," or the idea that due to the potential for great social mobility (in comparison to the European nations with which he was more familiar), any individual could become economically and socially successful, regardless of the social class to which they were born. However, even the most cursory examination of economic mobility "shows there is far less of it than economists once thought and less than most people believe" (Scott & Leonhardt 2005, 2), demonstrating why the American Dream is indeed a "dream" rarely realized upon waking.

On the other hand, de Tocqueville warned of the potential for egoism and selfishness to become inherent in such individualistic systems. When an individual's hard work is wholeheartedly believed to result in financial success and financial success is proof of that individual's hard work, then Americans may become locked into the constant pursuit of individual financial success (i.e., the "rat race") and blinded to the plight of their fellow citizens. Differences in success are expected, but these differences are framed individually. The master narrative does not contain stories that encourage differences to be viewed as collectively, structurally, or systematically. Another way to examine this hyper-individualizing effect is to consider the redemptive self-story. McAdams (2006) argued that those with merit are destined to give back. Yet, if individuals never come to believe they have merit because they are not *yet* successful, the focus becomes purely on the self.

The American Dream, both in its potential to engender values associated with success and its hyper-individualizing nature, continues to hold precedence as a cultural master narrative. However, it is important to note that the Dream is defined in ways entangled with capitalist consumer goals, including financial aspirations such as attending college (without crippling student debt), buying a home, raising a family, affording health care, and managing to save for retirement. How did this focus on finances occur? When originally coined, the American Dream signified a broad belief that individuals, without reference to their social class or economic background, could achieve success, defined as economic freedom, personal freedom, life, liberty, and the pursuit of happiness. In the aftermath of the Stock Market Crash of 1929 and the onset of the Great Depression, the American Dream narrative evolved, ultimately defining success more tightly with economic prosperity (Cullen 2003). Taken up by federal and state policy makers and intentionally marketed to Americans, the American Dream narrative was used to spur the economic recovery that promised a brighter financial future through individual hard work and individual effort.

Further, this promise of economic prosperity was incentivized by the American government. President Roosevelt's New Deal and the National Housing Act (1934) provided affordable homes and home mortgages for White men, establishing a widely accepted marker of economic success and fulfillment. Of note, prior to the Great Depression, it was rare for Americans (even middle-class citizens) to own their own homes (Chevan 1989). In 1944, the GI Bill continued to support home ownership as essential to the American Dream simultaneously establishing college education as an additional economic marker of success. This policy further subsidized the American Dream by affording White men returning from World War II the opportunity to get a free education and government-backed home loans. By designing federal policy that would allow White men previously shut out of the American Dream to access it, the GI Bill established a strong, White middle class. Mettler writes,

> Prior to 1940, colleges were mostly for the privileged, but the G.I. Bill opened doors to many Catholic and Jewish including rural people, first generation immigrant offspring, and veterans from working- and middle-class backgrounds. (2012, 1)

Designing policies that afforded opportunity where it did not previously exist made possible the successful attainment of the American Dream, particularly for poor and working-class White men. The systemic impact of such policy continues to impact the wealth of White America in today's economy (Katznelson 2005). Thus, opportunity and access in the US consumer markets became intimately connected to how Americans understand both their success and their constitutionally guaranteed rights of life, liberty, and pursuit of happiness (Cullen 2003). However, pursuit of such goals is highly individualized. As de Tocqueville warned, differential access and opportunity has resulted in a type of privileged egoism, or "tunnel vision," about the degree to which fellow citizens are able to make progress toward or achieve success. In fact, Americans may be unaware of the ways in which the American Dream has intentionally, both historically and today, functioned as a means of maintaining privilege. Adams wrote that the American Dream is "that dream of a land in which life should be better and richer and fuller for everyone, with opportunity for each according to ability or achievement" (1931, 214–215). Better for everyone does not mean opportunity for all, but rather *opportunity for each according to ability or achievement*. The narrative denies a collective lens. This intentional positioning protects privilege while denying the lived experiences of oppressed groups.

In 1935, Langston Hughes wrote the poem "Let America Be America Again" that juxtaposed the concept of the American Dream with the lived experiences of those socially and economically oppressed because of race, socioeconomic class, culture, or religion. Hughes's poem recognizes that America never epitomized the Dream in his poem. He writes,

(There's never been equality for me,
Nor freedom in this "homeland of the free.")

Say, who are you that mumbles in the dark?
—Excerpt, from "Let American Be America Again," by Langston Hughes

Importantly, Hughes's poem highlights that the American Dream was never intended for poor Whites, Blacks, Native Americans, or immigrants, despite the fact that individuals from these groups may have obtained various measures of success. Hughes's work highlights continued and sustained marginalization that is ignored in favor of the singular, individual stories that our history books and educational system emphasize as shining examples of what happens when hard work meets education.

Meritocratic Myths and School Accountability

We argue that there is a fundamental problem when access to guaranteed rights are not freely given, but instead, exchanged for opportunities earned in a meritocratic system. We are not the first to argue that the American Dream is more myth than reality. Where we intend to add to this argument is through critique of how the American merit narrative functions in schools to support and maintain the status quo (including systemic barriers) that act to prevent youth and their educators from real access to educational success.

For example, in 1964, President Johnson implemented the Great Society as an attempt to boost access for those who experienced limited opportunities to obtain the American Dream due to poverty and racial inequity. Perhaps the most far-reaching Great Society programming was the Elementary and Secondary Education Act (ESEA). The goal of ESEA was to give students "hope" by providing schools with additional resources targeted to close economic gaps between what students had and what they needed to be successful. Johnson signed ESEA into law in his hometown of Johnson City, Texas, a rural community, and invited his elementary school teacher to be with him (Goldstein 2014). He stated,

> By passing this Bill, we bridge the gap between helplessness and hope for more than 5 million educationally deprived children. And we rekindle the revolution—the revolution of the spirit against the tyranny of ignorance. As the son of a tenant farmer, I know that education is the only valid passport from poverty. As a former teacher—and, I hope, a future one—I have great expectations of what this law will mean for all of our young people. (Goldstein 2014, 114)

ESEA dollars continue to attempt to close opportunity gaps through ongoing professional development, curriculum materials, programming and parental engagement (Jeffrey 1978). ESEA has been reauthorized every five years since its inception under different policy names, including No Child Left Behind (NCLB) and Every Child Succeeds Act (ESSA), and with support from other federal policies such as Race to the Top (RTTT).

Prior to the early 2000s, federal policy in education was framed through a systemic (i.e., poverty focused) lens that, though far from perfect, attempted to create more opportunity for more people. Before 2001, federal dollars were targeted to create access where structuralized inequities and barriers limited access to the American Dream. These policies were designed to create opportunity or as Johnson stated, "to bridge the gap between helplessness and hope." If education was to be the bridge then it would be built by educators in the educational system and backed by moral and financial support of federal policy makers and the US government.

We highlight this history because of its significance to understanding the stories educators tell students today. Through the institution of schooling and related public policies, the American Dream narrative is maintained across generations, continually inculcating youth in a codified meritocracy in which they are led to believe they will be able to achieve economic mobility through their individual hard work and perseverance, despite the inequitable educational systems that prepared them for such work in the economic system (Cullen 2003).

In fact, the centrality of the American Dream master narrative makes race, gender, and class invisible as the spotlight is continually shown on the meritocratic elements of individual success stories. In education, critical race theory (CRT) offers a counter perspective that "emphasizes the centrality of race, racism, and White supremacy in describing educational structures and social practice" (Ladson-Billings & Tate 1995; Yosso 2005, 180). CRT perspectives contrast mainstream perspectives precisely because they counter "the hegemonic condition of the myth of meritocracy that leads individuals to believe that racism—as a structural barrier—is nonexistent" (Carter 2008, 15). Portraiture, a CRT methodology that centers the power of storytelling, attempts to keep the spotlight on systemic inequities that are washed out of stories that fit the cultural master narrative. Portraitists and scholars demonstrate a commitment to social action through sharing stories of successes or failures that are contextually fuller than the simplified cultural narratives (Chapman 2007).

Despite this, it is important to consider the degree to which the merit narrative remains especially pervasive in our cultural beliefs about the generative responsibilities we have to provide youth with educational opportunity so that they may become successful. Educators may feel this generative responsibility especially keenly as they have taken up professional responsibility to ensure student success, but the degree to which merit is confounded with academic achievement is widespread in American culture. In fact, the same GALEWiLL Center (2012) study that indicated the centrality of hard work to American beliefs about success showed that access to great schools (86 percent) and individual academic achievement (62 percent) are important precursors to achieving the American Dream.

It is therefore not coincidental that the Civil Rights Movement became so tied up in school settings. Landmark cases like *Brown v Board of Education* (1954) not only attempted to provide equal educational opportunity for all students but also codified the cultural emphasis on schools as sites to begin seeking the American Dream. Even after a generation of critique (e.g., Bell, 2005), schools are continuing to be seen as the great equalizer that allow students from different race and class backgrounds opportunities for success.

This is because so many American school policies have been designed around an overly simplified causal relationship between hard work, perseverance, and economic success (Weis 2008). In fact, the US politics of the last two decades of educational accountability are situated in using schools as the site in which individual merit is identified, hard work is demonstrated, and academic achievement will follow. Individual students' academic qualifications are quantified (e.g., high test scores, grade point averages, and graduation rates) and become the measures of high-performing schools. With the adoption of No Child Left Behind (2001), education federal policy shifted from addressing the systemic effects of poverty to focusing more closely on evidence of individual effort. School accountability became more aligned with the meritocratic narrative because policy measures no longer focused on the larger system. Instead, policy measures focused on individuals (school leaders, teachers, students) as evaluated by the measurable gains individual students made. Educational policy that had evolved to create "the anticipated charm of success" through programs for children in low-income housing, equal rights for women students and those with disabilities, vocational education, gifted and talented education, and even the Teacher Corps, began instead to focus on accountability measures that included the possible loss of funding, the risk of state take over, and competing for grants to enact educational policies. Federal policies placed responsibility for success firmly on the shoulders of individuals.

In schools today, accountability metrics continue to place the emphasis on individual students' achievement and teachers are held responsible for ensuring each individual student meets or exceeds expected achievement gains. Whether framed through as leaving no child left behind, racing to the top, or every student succeeding, the path to success and upward mobility is currently placed on the shoulders of students who see it as their responsibility to compete, work hard, and put forth their best effort despite overwhelming odds. Gone are the days when policy was designed to address structural barriers and historical injustices. Instead, individual ability, one's own talent coupled with hard work and perseverance, is central to obtaining success in schools and by extension, the American Dream.

Such neoliberal ideologies about the economic purposes of schooling result in ever greater competitiveness (Brantlinger 2003). Schools soon become treated like businesses, with stiff capitalistic competition for access to good schools that have demonstrated the ability to graduate successful students. In the end, little attention is paid to school inequity. Brantlinger further argues that school accountability professionals have conspired with middle- and upper-class parents to maintain inequities. School choice, voucher programs, tax credits, and educational savings accounts have resulted in a proliferation of charters, magnets, virtual schools, and other capitalistic alternatives to publicly provided schools, all aimed at providing equitable (i.e., better) opportunities for some students than others. It is no surprise that some children are advantaged because their families have the resources or social capital to take advantage of the schooling system. In fact, the 2019 "Varsity Blues" scandal in which parents were embroiled in a number of bribery and cheating scandals to ensure their children had better than equal access to college education was more surprising in that parents faced criminal charges than that they were scheming to take advantage of the meritocratic system in schools.

Like de Tocqueville, we argue there is both a positive spin to the myth and a negative outcome to the reality. Schools are seen as places that prepare students to reach the American Dream (i.e., a generative goal of supporting the next generation). Yet, schools also reward accountability metrics that are meant to identify talent and hard work, thus reinforcing systems of meritocracy that we want to believe measure an individual's "anticipated success."

At the same time, we cannot avoid the realizing that what may work for students in better schools (i.e., privileged, White students in middle- and upper-class well-resourced suburban schools and alternatives) does not also work for students in worse schools (i.e., underprivileged students of color and poverty in urban and rural schools). It is through hyper-individualizing the meritocratic myth that structural and systemic barriers in education are rendered invisible. By placing full emphasis on individual talent and hard work, the salience of privilege and lack of privilege become lost. Liu writes,

> A troubling effect of an uncritical view of meritocracy is that by not acknowledging there are greater structural social inequalities at play, there may be a tendency to view students who do not reach higher levels of educational attainment as having failed on their own terms. (2011, 384)

As with economic success, if Americans buy into the myth that potential and hard work are demonstrated through achievement and accountability data, and achievement and accountability data are proof of students' hard work, then families become locked into the constant pursuit of academic success and are blinded to the plight of students whose hard work does not result in achievement. It becomes all too easy to blame a lack of success on a lack of effort.

THE STORIES EDUCATORS TELL

We believe that American educators too often tell redemptive self-stories in service of the meritocratic master narrative. Redemptive self-stories, at least when the overall narrative is one of perceived success, motivate educators to engage in generative goals (i.e., by supporting the next generation of students). However, when an individual's overall narrative is one in which they do not see themselves as successful (yet), they may become self-focused and caught up in individual demonstrations of meritocratic values such as publicizing their hard work and perseverance. In either case, the tendency to see their own successes and failures through the lens of the master narrative has the consequence of focusing their efforts on individual students, ascribing merit to those who achieve success through hard work and perseverance, and failure to those who have not achieved success seemingly through a lack of effort or perseverance.

We agree there are potential benefits in supporting individual and prosocial values and argue there are potential drawbacks in hyper-individualizing to the extent that structural and systemic issues go unexamined. In particular, Loose (2008) reminds us that little research has been conducted on the impact of the individualistic focus in US schools. For example, we know from the literature that US students are taught to be "independent" thinkers and to treat achievement as competition (e.g., Trumbull, Rothstein-Fisch, & Hernandez 2003). In response, educators design curriculum and classrooms that focus on "the individual and emphasize individual responsibility for learning" (Loose 2008, 119). The result is that education systems are hyper-individualized and reinforce individualism as a core belief.

Likewise, we argue that schools are a site in which such stories are told and retold to foster individual hard work and perseverance and to motivate the next generation of students toward reaching the American Dream. Educators are uniquely positioned to contribute to this storytelling. For example, schools teach local histories and tell stories of local heroes that serve as examples that meritocracy works in contexts familiar to the students (e.g., students in Detroit hear stories about the hard work of Henry Ford, while students in Pittsburgh hear about the obstacles Andrew Carnegie overcame).

However, as educational advocates, we are especially interested in school stories that go beyond the individual to address social justice.

Despite a need to disrupt school narratives that result in individual critiques of student effort, the normative, internalized, and reproduced master narrative is difficult to question, particularly when educators tell their own stories in ways consistent with the master narrative and when familiarity with cultural storytelling makes it easy to call to mind examples of individuals who are successful. Despite clear evidence that the central tenets of the narrative are mythic (i.e., idealized), those who have "made it" continue to understand themselves through the lens of the cultural master narrative. When the American Dream myth interacts with the meritocracies inherent in US schooling, teachers who have "made it," courtesy of their own education, believe they are supporting youth by supporting hard work and perseverance in education. To think otherwise is constructed as un-American.

Context of the Storytelling

To be clear, we did not enter this work to investigate the meritocratic stories of educators. Rather, we were interested in how educators' understandings of themselves and their students as courageous shaped the work they undertook as social justice advocates in schools. We questioned how educators saw their work as challenging the systemic and structural barriers students of color and students of poverty faced in their classrooms. However, when asked *explicitly* about courage, the educators told stories of success as arising from the courage to work hard and persevere over obstacles. Therefore, work that was originally framed as an exploration of how to support teachers to be courageous led us instead to interrogate the success stories educators tell in schools and to our most vulnerable students. In addition, we learned about how educators lean into the master narrative in order to sustain what they do in schools.

Stories and Narratives as Methodology

This work uses storytelling as a methodology to understand conceptual systems, perceptions of identity, and the ways cultural metaphors are enacted in practice. Consistent with the telling and retelling of stories, we use a journey line protocol in our data collection. A journey line is a "story of self" protocol that allows participants to identify important moments (i.e., stories) in their own histories and to explore the ways they link together to form a personal narrative. A journey line uses an individual's experience(s) as a moving force for reflection and change (Dewey 1938). The individual and collective experience(s) as remembered and retold by participants works to build an aggregate story, or a narrative. In this way, an individual's (re)told stories can be used to construct a "story of self" that comprise a narrative of well-remembered plot points from childhood to present.

Important to our decisions to engage with this methodology is the idea that journey lines, when shared, become the "story of us" and can become a "story of collective knowledge or action" about a particular topic. In addition, an individual or a community may come together to form journey lines that support a specific purpose or an area of inquiry. For example, journey lines of courage, change, or advocacy may be built by individuals or communities. By charting the development change from childhood through the present, storytellers are able to identify themes and barriers to their practice. Using this aspect, Guajardo, Guajardo, Janson, & Militello (2015) use journey lines to support and sustain socially just actions in personal and professional development.

As noted, the journey lines constructed by educators presented in these chapters were framed around the central construct of "courage" as we believe this to be a necessary element to support and sustain when working with social justice advocates in schools. In short, we believe that empowered teachers empower students to overcome barriers and reach their full potential. This framing was consistent with the professional development goals we were helping to support. Namely, the educators were seeking to challenge and change systems that resulted in inequities for students of color and students of poverty in their school settings. In engaging with journey line methodology, we were seeking to better understand the personal and professional narratives that support and impede professional development for advocacy for social justice in schools. Specifically, these educators were involved in a professional development experience to see, name, challenge, and change unjust norms and practices in order to increase access and opportunity for children of color and children of poverty in their school settings.

The Educators

We share here the stories of six educators, four teachers and two school social workers. Four of the educators identified as women of color (three African American women and one Japanese woman) and two as White men. Consistent with McAdams (2006) work, five of the six were in a generative stage of life (thirties to fifties), while one woman was slightly younger.

As a group, they work in schools in a mid-Atlantic urban center. Like many such areas in the United States, this city supported a thriving middle-class with industrial work. As industry declined, the demographics of the neighborhoods shifted. The educators in this study work in schools built to service White, middle-class, suburban families. Now these schools serve primarily children of color and children in poverty. In fact, the student population is commonly referred to as disadvantaged, marginalized, and at-risk. Although this labeling resulted in funding for the professional development these educators were involved in, we are also deeply aware of the ways in which "language is not an innocent reflection of how we think. The terms we use control our perceptions, shape our understanding, and lead us to particular proposals for improvement" (Milner 2008, 1574). Importantly, Milner's argument is consistent with the meritocratic master narrative. In particular, he highlights the hyper-individualizing of these students, namely that such labels "are used as adjectives to describe students and other individuals in the learning community rather than the institutional, bureaucratic, or systemic situations that are in place and used to maintain the status quo" (Milner 2008, 1574). Therefore, we wish to make clear that the educators we describe here were social justice advocates, but also that they were successful in funding this professional development opportunity because they were able to frame their students in a particular way, as "disadvantaged, marginalized and at risk."

Storytelling: Journey Lines and Interviews

Each educator completed a journey line of their courage in schools. The written journey line helped support the educators to recall stories and develop a cohesive narrative. The themes we present here derive from follow-up semi-structured interviews to explore the educators' stories and how their personal narratives influence their advocacy work in schools.

As qualitative researchers, we are interested in how:

> the storied qualities of qualitative textual data, both "naturally" given or research driven, enable the analyst to consider both how social actors order and tell their experiences and why they remember and retell what they do. The structuring of experience can hence be analyzed alongside meanings and motives. (Coffey & Atkinson 1996, 57)

We argue that the initial journey line acted as structuring experience, with the follow-up interview providing the educators with the opportunity to reflect upon their stories. In retelling their stories and sharing their narratives, they came to define courage in schools and were able to share personally influential moments of courage.

Analysis

Interviews were audio recorded, transcribed, and de-identified prior to descriptive/interpretative analysis. Rather than analyze responses by interviewer question, we chose to analyze transcripts holistically (i.e., as stories told rather than responses to prompts). We initially sought to better understand educator definitions of courage in schools, but we quickly found it necessary to adopt a grounded theory approach (Glaser & Strauss 1967), whereby themes and categories arose as we worked through the responses. No a priori codes were used. Instead, as thematic codes arose, emergent descriptions were recorded along with examples. The developing codebook was then subjected to peer debriefing (Marshall & Rossman 2006) in order to ensure themes were reflective of the educators' stories and narratives and not driven by the initial framing of courage or awareness of the professional development experiences. Once theme descriptions were finalized, transcripts were independently coded. All coding disagreements were resolved in discussions between the researchers.

Themes

The following four themes arose from educators' shared stories and reflected on their overall narratives to make sense of their work as educators and social justice advocates. Although initially surprising given the framing of our interest and procedures around courage, the educators overwhelmingly shared stories consistent with the cultural master narrative of meritocracy. The first two hyper-individualized themes we present emphasize this. In contrast, a small subset of stories focused more on the collective and the system than on the individual educator or student. The last two themes we present emphasize this alternate storytelling.

Hard Work and Perseverance

Within the theme of hard work and perseverance, educators shared several kinds of stories. When telling stories about their students, they focused on obstacles they believed could be overcome with perseverance and success stories about students they felt exemplified the meritocratic values of hard work and perseverance. They also retold stories that were framed in such a way to give advice to students about these values. Finally, they told personal stories of their own successes as having resulted from hard work and perseverance. The following sections provide examples of each of these types of shared stories.

First, educators recognized ways in which their students were particularly "at risk" in pursuing their educations and told stories of obstacles in current circumstances and contexts that the educators believed required hard work and perseverance to overcome. For example, one woman educator described her student population as:

> I got a kid that was once homeless. I have kids who have lost, you know, who might have lost loved ones. I have kids who have watched their mothers struggle with their sexual identity. I have kids—I mean I could go on and on about how they actually—it's a confession, I mean they are . . . they are crying.

Similarly, another educator reflected on how he had come to be more understanding of student's "bad" behaviors as he came to better understand the obstacles his students were facing. For example, he perceived himself to be "tough" on absenteeism or sleeping during class early in his career. However, he reflected that he now tries to find ways to support these students because

> Every one of them has different challenges, and it seems that we didn't even consider . . . There are kids that are doing very poorly in class, maybe cutting class, maybe fall asleep, or whatever. You kind of get mad at them because they are not doing the things that they are supposed to do. And then you find out later on that they are actually taking care of two or three younger brothers or sisters all night while mom or dad are working—and they are getting them dinner, and they are getting them dressed, and putting them to bed—and then they stop to do their own work! And so they are up late at night and then trying to come to school functioning.

Responses such as these showed educators learning about their students' lives outside of the classroom. They reflected on particular students who had helped them to realize the incongruence between the "good" student behaviors associated with a "strong work ethic" and accountability and achievement pressures and the real-life obstacles their students face.

The educators clearly perceived conflicts between real-life struggles and classroom expectations. However, the stories also exemplify the hyper-individualism of the meritocratic master narrative. As seen in these examples, the obstacles and barriers described by the educators were specific to individual students. The educators rarely described obstacles in systemic or structural ways. And, in fact, their stories of courageous students suggested expectations for students to work hard, despite their community's collective circumstances.

Second, the educators shared "success" stories of particularly "courageous" students who had demonstrated significant hard work and perseverance in the face of extreme circumstances. For example, when asked to recount examples of student courage, one man responded,

> I know that I have some students that were not coming out to school for a while. When they come back, and I say, "You missed a couple of days." And you find out they were afraid to leave their house because there was a shooting in the neighborhood, three or four doors down! So for some of them it takes courage to leave the house . . . You know you have to put that into perspective. So okay, what really is important here?

Although the educators seemed to understand that the obstacles their students faced were often due to overwhelming individual circumstances (e.g., a mother's addiction) or systemic inequities (e.g., neighborhood violence and lack of resources in the schools), the narrative of individual hard work and perseverance leading to success was used to frame nearly all of the successful stories they shared. For example, one educator shared a story of a student he found to be particularly courageous:

> He was heavy into drugs, mom OD'd, and there were just a lot of problems, and his grades were already slipping. And we talked every single day (And it took about half an hour out of my day, every single day to talk to him!), but he drove his grades up to like a 3.5. He's looking at becoming a nurse, which . . . I guess he's been staying with a friend. I could not imagine having to leave your family 'cause life is so bad! So I think he's staying with a friend only because he knows it's the only way to be able to concentrate and worry about his life ahead really. And . . . I think that takes a lot of courage to be the person—again I'm not, I wouldn't think that deep into it, you know—to be able to tell your mother, "I'm leaving here."

As seen in this story, the teacher is impressed with the student's courage to persevere despite his family's struggles, all the while working hard to prioritize his individual success.

Third, stories about specific students were shared in much the same way as their own stories were shared—as a means of demonstrating the meritocratic values they wanted students to embrace. For example, one teacher recalled a moment from her journey line that she shares with students,

> by the time I got to high school it . . . Just again, it was, "You remember this," and "You write this," and worksheet after worksheet. And my mom said, "Listen this is your life. I'm not going to put you on punishment anymore. You have to do what you need to do." And I made the choice to go to college . . . and, I hated it . . . And then I thought I was just going to be a nothing, a nobody! But my parents were like, "You're going to finish school! I don't know what you're going to major in, but you're going to finish!" And then I transferred. I transferred four times! And I met a lady on the elevator. I remember it to this day. She asked me what I was majoring in, and I told her, "I just don't know!" [laughter] She said, "Well, dear, why are you here?" And I said, "Because I have to be!" And she said, "I would like for you to take one of my classes." And I took one of her classes, and it was an education class, and I loved it. It was hands-on, and I just remember saying, "Wait—I can do this?"

A similar story was shared by another woman, who attempted to inspire her students to work hard and persevere in order to demonstrate merit to others.

> It's something that will never leave me. I want to say I was in eighth grade, and it was my Nana (my dad's mom). And she told me I was never going to be nobody—"Never going to be anything! Just like your mother! You look like your mother! You act just like your mother!" And I internalized that. I still do. I think about that. It always sits at the

back of my head. Her saying that helped me get through my master's program. I ended up going to get my Master's in Science (something I could have done years ago, but didn't, because I didn't want to take the math classes), and every time I wanted to quit, I could hear her in my ear. And I'm really open with my class. I'm really open with my students, and I told them that. I shared that part of me, you know, with them—that "There was once this person who . . . Hold onto that, because they will feed you!" . . . Every time that I feel that I can't do any more (if I want to give up), I think about those words, and it helps me get through . . . It allows for me to continue on and it helps me also to motivate my students to want more.

In fact, the educators often reflected on stories from their journey lines that they argued demonstrated personal courage because they had persevered over circumstances that were perceived to be unfair to them individually. For example, in reflecting on his journey line, one man commented,

My moment of courage was when I was younger, working in a hardware store. Again, people would pass me up for the older person. Yet they did not always have the knowledge that I actually had of the product, of the services that were available there, and that has always been in the back of my head while teaching.

This teacher explicitly connected his own experience of persevering through perceived age discrimination with his students' need to persevere in school systems that "stereotype" them based on their race, class, or school track, stating "you do have some low-level students, and you have such high level students, and you have the middle of the road students. That's really challenging, and that's where stereotyping can come in real quickly." Despite acknowledging the systemic schooling issues, the solution he advocated for was individual hard work and perseverance. The teacher also believed he was able to forge a connection with these students through his own example. In effect, he relied on the shared meritocracy narrative to connect his own successes to the potential for success for his students:

Again, a lot of our students have a very rough home life. And again, we have these conversations every day between me and maybe three of my students—just about careers, about life, about issues that are in their lives and how I can connect to them. Again, the connection always does go back to that because I tell them that I've worked in a hardware store for twelve years. You have to work to get what you want, and when things are given these days to a lot of kids, a lot of families, a lot of people these days, it's hard for them to see that if you work hard, you can do very well in life. And I think that's probably the biggest message that I have, because I know the hard work that goes into things, of not being given anything. Coming from a low middle-class family that we didn't have much growing up either, but I wanted the most out of life.

In short, across all the examples of stories the educators told about their students and about themselves, the recipe for success was hard work and perseverance.

Therefore, it was not surprising that educators also described more generally how they either "push" or "support" their students to be "courageous" and "work hard" when faced with difficulties or obstacles. For example, one woman educator stated, "By giving them the little bit of courage, you can say, 'Hey, you can do this if you put your mind to it!'" Another women shared,

> I try to instill in them that if they kind of step out of their own comfort zone a little bit, and try some things, and if they will be an advocate for themselves, that there's nothing really that they can't do. Because there's a lot of stuff out there that they are capable of doing, a lot of challenges that they are able to overcome, but they have to be confident within themselves and be willing to try. Life wouldn't be successful all the time . . . but it teaches you to be courageous and actually persevere through some of the stuff. And they have every right as all the other kids in all the school districts that have all this money to be afforded these opportunities.

Finally, educators connected these messages explicitly to their professional identities in explaining how they were professionally and personally invested in student success. For example, one educator drew explicit connections between her own success and that of her students, stating, "I have to push them to be successful, because that is the only way I'll be successful." Thus, the theme of hard work and perseverance carried across journey line narratives and shared stories, despite framing the prompts and questions around courage.

Identifying and Supporting Individual Talent

Responses in the second theme suggest that the participating educators saw their role within the school-based meritocratic narrative as helping students to discover individual talents and abilities that set them apart and would allow them to become successful (i.e., demonstrate merit). For example, one woman shared, "When they have an asset or treasure, they don't even know they have it. So to have someone recognize what they . . . Or to have someone point out, 'You have this.' 'Oh I didn't even know I had that.'" In this way, asset-based thinking and language was focused on students' individual skills, achievements, or treasures. Similarly, another woman teacher reflected that her primary motivational strategy was to help students identify their individual merits,

> Well, one thing I try to do is instead of focusing on what they can't do, focus on what they can do by getting to know my students and focusing on what they can do and what motivates them to learn. I use that as leverage, you know. I use that to help them when they can't get through—when they say "Ms. [Name], I can't do this," or "I don't understand that"—I try to always take it back to the things that they are good at, because I do believe that everybody sitting in my classroom is good at something.

On the one hand, we appreciate how these shared stories were full of hope. The educators firmly believed that every student had something at which they excel and that cultivating that skill would allow each individual student to overcome their current circumstances. They wanted students to focus on these abilities and to feel encouraged, rather than to focus on failures. However, we also worry. The stories that were shared framed teachers as treasure hunters. Their vocation was to find and unbury hidden talent and polish it up for sale in a capitalistic market. This strategy focused on making students aware of their skills and then encouraging them to work hard and to persevere to develop them. Systemic and structural inequities were not referenced in the majority of stories, or when they were, they were framed as something that could be overcome with sheer perseverance.

In speaking with the educators, most success stories were clearly about an individual protagonist (themselves or their students) who overcame obstacles through hard work, perseverance, and application of talent. When they spoke of their concerns, they identified individual students who face difficult individual, structural, or systemic challenges that would be significantly difficult to overcome. Yet, the suggested strategy remained hard work, perseverance, and application of individual talent.

Advocacy and Navigation

While most stories were well aligned with the cultural meritocratic master narrative, some more clearly spoke about the structural and systemic barriers in schools. In a subset of stories, the women of color clearly described inequities students faced, and they shared stories in which they had exemplified courage by actively advocating on behalf of their students as well as teaching students to navigate through challenging school systems or policies that were unjust. Most of these stories centered on student "voice," and educators shared how they supported students to be courageous and speak up for themselves. As befitting the professional development experiences that intended to assist educators to "see, name, challenge, and ultimately change, unjust norms and practices within their schools," the educators likewise provided "safe spaces" for students to see, name, and challenge by empowering student voice in their schools.

For example, one woman described how she uses a "Trigger Wall" to provide safe space for students to discuss difficult issues:

> I see them advocating for themselves as students through their writing about students having voices. They believe in student voice because I've allowed for them to have a voice. When we have a Trigger Wall, when we feel triggered, you know, they put their triggers on the wall so that everybody can see that, you know.

Likewise, in telling the story of "family meetings" she holds with students to help teach young women of color to navigate systems of inequity in schools, another educator described the following:

> I'm constantly talking to them about how to appropriately advocate for themselves, so that they don't come across as defiant or disrespectful. And I had a young lady one time come to me—She was angry she had tears in her eyes. And she told me everything she wanted to say, and then asked me how she could say it. [laughter] "I know I can't say it this way. How can I say this?" And we sat and we worked through it so that she could go back and voice her opinion and her concern without finding herself in trouble or receiving disciplinary action for her message.

Despite these strategies, the woman also explicitly recognized the power differentials in schools, and that students may not always be free to speak their truth. For example, one woman stated, "I try to use those feelings in my interactions with students to provide safe spaces for them to navigate those situations where they may not feel as secured or courageous." They took care to help students present their experiences in ways that would not have them "facing disciplinary action."

Protection

Finally, the educators referenced their own power and privilege in school spaces and shared stories about how they attempted to protect their students. Protection was coded when educators worried about the potential for students to be physically or emotionally endangered in school spaces. For example, in describing physical dangers, one man was adamant that, "I really give them a lot of credit because some of the kids, some of them tell me, 'I'm terrified to try this!' And 'As long you do exactly what I tell you, and show you to do, you'll never have a problem.'" The other man described the importance of students learning to trust in the teacher's protection, asserting, "Students trust me enough that they are not going to . . . that they are not going to be injured and they're going to be fine."

The women of color likewise argued for the importance of establishing a safe environment in which students trust the teacher to protect them, even when the dangers they face are not physical. For example, one teacher argued,

> Because kids learn in different ways. And I know the type of learner that I was. It just seemed that nobody really cared. I spend a lot of time getting to know my students. I don't believe that trust is something that you have to give. Trust is something that is earned, and my students don't begin to trust me until after Christmas. And I don't begin to trust them too until after Christmas, you know. Once you know a child, you begin to take the time to get to know them, you can teach them anything. But if you don't take that time to get to know them, you're just wasting your time. Now my kids can hold onto my every word and put it in a good way, not in a bad way. So even when I'm disciplining them, even when I'm screaming at them, they know there's a difference between talking to a kid and at a kid.

It was clear that in addition to creating "safe spaces" for advocacy, these educators wanted to make their classrooms safe and worked to protect students personally. They wanted students to trust them (individual relationships), but they also maintained rigid controls in their classrooms seemingly in an attempt to protect them from inequities within the system.

EDUCATOR STORIES AND NARRATIVES: SOME CONCLUSIONS AND IMPLICATIONS

The ways in which stories were told within larger narratives was particularly interesting in how courage and success were used interchangeably and noticeably aligned with the meritocratic master narrative when speaking about students. Educators described themselves as teaching students to be courageous/successful when they (a) supported students to discover their individual talents or (b) encouraged students to work hard(er) and persevere. These same themes were demonstrated in stories they told to us and to their students about the courage that resulted in their past successes and achievements. In contrast, they saw themselves as courageous in the profession when they (a) protected students by providing safe spaces in classrooms or (b) advocated for students in their schools or helped students navigate inequitable school systems to advocate for themselves. Thus, the data are best represented by a matrix as presented in table 2.1.

Once the data were mapped in this way and transcripts were identified by gender and race, it became clear that while all participants valued the meritocratic themes of hard work and perseverance to some extent (i.e., all educators told stories linking success to hard work and perseverance), their responses tended to fall along the diagonals. To clarify, the women of color responded with similar themes across the stories they

Table 2.1. Revised Matrix of Educator Responses to Courage Prompts

Educator Responses	Themes	
I can teach students to be courageous and successful by . . . (engaging with meritocracy themes)	discovering and supporting students' individual talents and assets.	pushing them to work hard(er) and persevere over difficult circumstances, showing them that effort will have great rewards.
I can be courageous for students by . . . (engaging with schools as systems)	protecting and controlling classroom spaces to keep students safe.	advocating for students and helping students advocate for themselves in ways that will be effective.

told. They contextualized meritocratic stories by sharing how they support students by helping them identify their talents so that they can use these talents to navigate inequitable systems. Hard work and perseverance were described in service to special gifts or talents. Oftentimes, these stories were contextualized within their own experiences of inequity and how a mentor identified their special merits, which when paired with hard work and perseverance, allowed them to succeed. So, for example, the woman who spoke so emphatically about her belief that every student "has an asset and treasure" that she is able to find and support, explicitly connected these strengths as a means "to accommodate what might be missing." Her journey line stories reiterated these themes of support of talent and she connected specific stories (e.g., of one mentor identifying her own strengths as a mother at a time when she was struggling with economic barriers and another [White man] colleague praising her expertise and amplifying her ideas when she was struggling in a professional setting) to ideas of using individual talents to compensate for inequitable systems. Like this woman, the other women shared stories about how they were taught to see and navigate systems by mentors (i.e., these early personal moments of courage were noted on the journey lines and framed stories they told in the interviews). Additionally, they told multiple stories of targeted support through identifying and nurturing the talents of each individual student.

In contrast, the teachers who identified as White men primarily responded along the other diagonal. The journey lines of their personal moments of courage and their observations of their students' courage reflected "bright spots" stories with a tighter focus on the themes of hard work and perseverance over obstacles. The stories centered hard work and perseverance without either the individual context of talent/merit or the systemic context of inequitable barriers. For example, the same man told the story of the student who left home to focus on his education and the personal story of overcoming negative stereotypes about his age when he worked in retail. Like the other man, his personal moments of courage illustrated a view of himself as earning his success through working hard and perseverance rather than through application of any particular talent. Despite his earnest desire to help his students, he did not center the need to identify particular talents or navigate systems. His story did not reference his own privilege or how his experiences may differ from his students in systemic ways. Instead, he sought to draw direct parallels through shared experiences of successes born from hard work and perseverance. In turn, these teachers taught students to be courageous by instilling a work ethic that they believed would allow them to become successful. In contrast to the women of color who opened safe spaces for their students to voice and learn to navigate injustices, these men created safe spaces by maintaining tight control and setting limits in their classrooms to protect students and believed their role was to "take some of the worry out of it" so their students could have the freedom to explore and learn without danger.

A RETURN TO COURAGE

As you no doubt recall, the initial goal of this work was to better understand how to support and sustain educators' professional courage to engage in acts of advocacy in their schools. It was initially surprising that educators defined courage as so completely aligned with meritocratic themes, namely hard work and perseverance over obstacles. In particular, courage was defined as demonstrating more and harder work than peers demonstrate. In short, educators considered themselves to be examples of professional courage when trying new things and going beyond expectations of what they expected from other teachers or what they believed was expected of them by their principals. For example, one woman of color said,

> Professional courage would be stepping out, to go above and beyond your comfort zone within your career field or your area of expertise . . . if you're doing this grant and doing some of the other outside activities, it takes you out of that comfort zone..So I really think that in terms of stepping out and going out of your content area . . . I think that could be a really scary thing.

Examples of "stepping out" included continually adapting instruction, year after year or for particular students, and seeking professional development and grant opportunities to better support their students. And importantly, these educators did not expect their colleagues to be courageous in the same ways they were. For example, one man told us,

> Like I said before, this is my twenty-ninth year, so I'm kind of on the down-slide. And for a lot of teachers, they wouldn't even consider

taking something on that would be this much work this late in their career! And so a lot of them want to just close the latch because of their other career. They don't want to change whatever they teach or how they teach. They just want to make it as simple as possible and kind of go out gracefully.

Thus, teachers reported that going beyond expectations was courageous because they perceived a lack of institutional interest or support for their continued hard work, which is particularly unsettling given the way they value hard work and perseverance. As one woman explained, professional courage is necessary,

> because you are nervous to do something new. And especially when you don't have a whole lot of support, and you are kind of on your own. You have to dive in, and examine, and just do it yourself. It's almost like getting down into the water and you have to swim. Like you buckle up and swim instead of saying, "I can't swim." So when I'm doing my project, that's what the courage is. And also when I'm doing my own work, the courage could mean looking for a perfect tool for me. Say like if you get thrown into the water, what is available to me that's going to help out? For example, I might have a great idea for something, but because I may feel that people may not value what I have to say, I would look for who can be an ally and spokesperson for me that people would respect and listen to. So, the courage means, the courage could mean buckling up and swimming by yourself and doing it yourself. At the same time, courage could mean looking for a tool or resource that is useful to me.

This literal "sink or swim" interpretation of courage demonstrates that educators felt that the chronic lack of support was a systemic barrier they needed to navigate or an obstacle over which they needed to persevere. For example, one woman of color reported that, "I think professional courage is being able to stand for what you believe, even if you are standing alone. And pushing through when you don't want to push through. And maybe pushing back when you would just prefer to give in." The alignment between their definitions of professional courage and their own perseverance was best exemplified in their journey line stories. For example, one of the men told a story about going beyond expectations when a physical resource (classroom space) was taken away from him:

> So, they told me I would have to move upstairs, but I moved into two smaller classrooms than what I had downstairs. So it's been a real challenge for me to try to function within about half of the amount of space. And so I had to adapt the room, and also adapt the way I do a lot of the things, just to be able to try and function within that space. So 30 days have been kind of a challenge. And every day, it's kind of too, just, kind of "suck it up" and do what I have to do to try to make this all function best as I can within that space.

This educator believed other teachers would not work as hard as he has to overcome the frustrating situation.

In addition to dealing with a lack of support that in terms of limited resources, educators similarly felt they were courageous when there was a lack of support for their skills and contributions. The following story demonstrates how one woman believed she demonstrated courage as a teacher by persevering over an institutional obstacle:

> Well, as a public education teacher being in the public system, we have the Union and of course the Union . . . I mean it's great to have, but in some instances it's not. And I will tell you when I started my program, the Union tried everything that they could to stop it from happening. (I have an after-school program. Courses are the same.) I was just up against so much, and at the end of the day, I just kept ploughing through. I had parents that supported me. I have 22 girls and a waiting list every year! So I know that I'm doing something right, regardless of what they say or may say.

Additionally, these educators' definitions and stories of their professional courage provide evidence of the day-to-day difficulties and frustrations of working in public schools.

Courageous Stories of Collective Action

It is within this context of ongoing lack of resources and systemic issues in schools that the need for collective action arose. Professional support happens every day, and is, according to one man, "Just helping one another, because there's a lot of rough days here. And just, this job comes with it. Helping one another, each teacher." Unlike the ways some educators attempted to identify and support specific individual strengths with their students, professional support was more about presence—just being there for their colleagues. As the previous teacher put it, "In this building everybody has each other's back." When asked how presence and support were part of professional courage, one woman replied,

> Courage takes one step at a time, and sometimes you don't even know when you're being courageous. I think . . . I think that most courage is, you don't know when you're being courageous. I think that the courage, when you step out, you're not thinking about anything else, you're just doing it for the love. And you're taking it one step at a time, and hoping that you're moving in the right direction. But a lot of times, you know, being courageous, someone else has to tell you that this took courage.

In contexts that lacked physical and institutional resources to support the daily efforts of teachers, these educators believed it was courageous to be in support of each other. Ironically, this is a story of wanting a collective experience as opposed to an individualistic one and demonstrates a need for alternatives to the meritocratic master narrative.

THREE
The Stories Students Tell

In this chapter, the stories of youth who worked with the educators described in chapter 2 are shared. As you read their stories, we ask you to consider the following questions: (1) How do students make sense of the narratives shared in their schools? (2) To what extent do students take up or place value on themes of these narratives in their own identities? (3) Where and when are opportunities to disrupt the myth of meritocracy present in the stories that youth tell?

The purpose of this chapter is to begin to uncover the degree to which the meritocratic master narrative permeates and burdens youth identity in US schools and to explore strategies for supporting the development of more fluid and multifaceted identities in school contexts, which in turn support strategic valuing of more diverse assets within school systems. Finally, by bringing together the educator and student stories, we begin to surface the complicated, complex, and communal stories we suspect are needed to sustain advocacy efforts in schools.

MERITOCRATIC MYTHS AND SCHOOL DISCOURSE

As you have read, meritocratic storytelling is incredibly pervasive in US culture, and we argue this plays out in problematic ways in schools where success is widely understood as a function of student work ethic. The language of merit in school systems is enticing because it signals to students that there is something unique about them that will allow them to succeed, while simultaneously blurring into the background structural inequities that may prevent some of their peers from doing the same. In most cases, students are not encouraged to examine assumptions about the way things are in schools and what should be valued, further masking unjust decisions and actions and the disparate patterns they create (Mishler 1995).

Nevertheless, educators and school systems have both historically and in modern times promoted stories to students that center the relationship between hard work, perseverance, and economic success (Weis 2008). Ris (2015) maps out a compelling argument that identifies "work ethic" as the concept historically used in US schools to motivate middle-class children to develop the character needed to translate school success to economic success (i.e., attainment of the American Dream). For example, he cites the classic Horatio Alger Jr. novels that feature "rags to riches" stories of impoverished boys who by the end of the story are able to become successful by securing respectable middle-class standing. Alger wrote more than a hundred novels that followed this script. Most feature a poor, White American boy whose work ethic (identified as hard work, perseverance, and conscientiousness to doing their best) and honesty bring him to the attention of a successful businessman who then assists the main character by starting him on an entrepreneurial path. Despite consistently featuring a disadvantaged youth as the main character, Ris (2015) argues that the stories were written for middle-class students who demonstrate their work ethic within a context of privilege (i.e., well-resourced schools) wherein the causal relationship between work ethic and success is not impeded by structural or systemic barriers. In fact, the "discourse is not driven by concern for disadvantaged students, but by the anxiety of middle- and upper-class parents about the character of their own children" (Ris 2015, 10).

In the same way, today's educators may invoke "grit." As a psychological construct, grit is defined as "perseverance and passion for long term goals. Grit entails working strenuously towards challenges, maintaining effort and interest over years despite failure, adversity, and plateaus in progress" (Duckworth 2016, 1087). Grit encapsulates the hard work, perseverance, conscientiousness, and resilience of work ethic with the addition of passion for a goal and courage in pursuit of it. Duckwork's research emphasizes grit as the hallmark of high achievers in every field, and we do not doubt the power of combining passion, hard work, and perseverance.

However, grit is taken up in modern schools with teachers exhorting their students to work hard(er) and persevere so that they can overcome obstacles to academic success. Gorski (2016) problematizes this usage in settings that serve children of poverty, critiquing the tendency of teachers to tell "gritty" stories about their own or their family's accomplishments in overcoming or avoiding economic hardships. The personal stories of educators, likely to be White middle class themselves, promote a false equivalence with their students and fail to reference a sophisticated understanding of the structural ideology of poverty. In understanding themselves to be gritty and therefore successful, teachers may embrace a deficit perspective in which poor students come from poor families who failed to work their way out of poverty as the educators and their families have done. Students who seemingly are exceptionally gritty in many aspects of their lives, given the obstacles educators described in the previous chapter, may not also become academically successful. If this occurs, such students will be viewed through the lens of the meritocratic master narrative as examples of a poor work ethic or a lack of grit.

Growth mindset (Dweck 2006) is taken up in schools in similar ways. Like grit and work ethic, a growth mindset is believed to be a means to achieve equity and empower children of color and children of poverty to be as successful as their more privileged peers (Generett & Olson 2020). We agree that a growth mindset has the potential to be very powerful in school settings. When teachers and students embrace a growth mindset (in contrast with a fixed or entity mindset), they believe that academic skills and the ability to learn academic content is not limited. They believe everyone has the ability to become more skilled with effort and perseverance. In other words, when students believe they can become smarter, they are motivated to put in more effort to learn, and this pays off in achievement. The growth mindset literature has been further bolstered in recent years with neuroscience findings about brain plasticity—essentially that with experience and practice, we can build new connections and strengthen existing connections in our brains.

Yet, like grit, there is a gulf between what the research says and how the stories are told in school. It is problematic that Dweck's work is incorrectly being used as a means to provide educators with additional language and metaphors to fold into narratives linking hard work, perseverance, and merit. Dweck (2006) acknowledges this, suggesting that the most common misconception in how growth mindset is enacted in schools is through equating growth mindset with effort. She writes, "Too often nowadays, praise is given to students who are putting forth effort, but not *learning*, in order to make them feel good in the moment . . . The growth mindset was intended to help close achievement gaps, not hide them" (Dweck 2006, 1). The critique, of course, is that even in this achievement gap language, the narrative remains deficit focused.

Dweck's commentary also highlights a key concern we share. Educators may justify why students are not learning by saying they have a fixed mindset, are not gritty enough, or do not work hard enough. The language may have changed since Horatio Alger Jr.'s novels, but the blame continues to be placed on the individual student's lack of work ethic. This hyper-individualizing is consistent with the meritocratic master narrative in that it places the responsibility for success squarely on the individual's shoulders. However, it fails to support students because little attention is paid to the inequitable distribution of resources students can bring to recovering from failure. For example, helping students to embrace a growth mindset looks different when there are school supplies (e.g., paper, pencils, access to computers) that allow students to keep trying than it does when there are not. Helping students try new strategies looks different when teachers have the freedom to set their own pacing than it does when teachers are held to a scripted curriculum or pacing guide. Put simply, continued and strategic effort may be met with success when appropriately resourced, but the same effort may be met with disappointment when time and resources are limited. If we use the same narratives in each setting, we set students (and teachers) up to feel angry and disappointed when they fail to be successful.

So while we value hard work, perseverance, passion, and the development of talent, we worry, based on the literature and the courageous stories educators told us, that the stories shared in schools overly simplify the relationship between these values and success. Motivating students is certainly worthwhile, but there is also need for caution when the push and pull of motivation is framed only or mostly through the values of meritocracy. When this happens, motivational theories are reduced to simpler metaphors that ultimately shape students' identities as learners and doers. For example, we have all been told to "put your back into it" and "keep your nose to the grindstone." We are warned to "keep trying" and "don't let them out work you." Difficult school work is equated to "blood, sweat, and tears" and we are never done, because there is "always room to improve." Rather than be strategic in putting our effort where it might do the most good, we are told to "always try your hardest" because "to give anything less than your best is to sacrifice the gift" (Steve Prefontaine, American Olympic Runner). Further, educators' awareness and understandings of the language they invoke, whether as more colorful metaphoric language or specifically as attempting to leverage work ethic, grit, or growth mindset, may not have depth, nor lead directly to plans for how to support students to be successful (Ullici & Howard 2015). Educator use of these framings may instead reify the cultural master narrative and associated values to (re)inscribe the values of "pull yourself up by your bootstraps," another metaphor historically used to place the responsibility of inequitable systems onto marginalized people. Similarly, when we notice school personnel take up these tropes without acknowledging the past and present-day impact of inequities, we wonder if we are setting students and teachers up to fail.

Further, the cultural values and mythic stories educators espouse may even directly contradict the ways in which real policies are enacted in schools to maintain existing meritocracies. For example, Oakes's (2005) pivotal work on tracking demonstrates ways in which school policies work to maintain both inequities and the status quo. Oakes makes clear the ways in which barriers students face vary in difficulty, navigability, and transparency, but that these variations are cloaked by the system of tracking. When students are separated for instruction based on individual ability or aptitude, this act of individualizing serves to underscore meritocratic themes about talent and hard work. In such systems, both successes and failures are the responsibility of the individual, whose needs are expected to be met by the system that provided them with educational experiences and opportunities at their individual levels.

REPETITION AND THE NEGATIVE IMPLICATIONS OF "COMMON SENSE"

We argue that the meritocratic master narrative and associated cultural values, though intended to serve White, middle class, privileged classes, may not serve any students well in reality, particularly because it is so normalized that it has become "common sense" in schools. As Kumashiro writes, "what we take to be 'common sense' is not something that just is; it is something that is developed and learned and perpetuated over time" (2008, 3). And, in fact, such meritocratic norms elevate the exceptional student as the model, while arguing every student can achieve to the same level. This is because what constitutes merit is dependent on school context, tracking, and a variety of other structures, but merit is communicated to students as if it is innate talents within individual students.

Moreover, as we saw with the educators' narratives in chapter 2 and as Liu explains, those who benefit from a meritocratic system, "believe they have earned whatever rewards they have come to possess" (2011, 386). Yet, the reverse is also true. When students do not achieve it is believed to be due to a lack of merit, an inadequate work ethic, and an inability to persevere and sustain one's best effort in the face of obstacles. In fact, this purposeful misidentification of norms for success is part of the design of the master narrative to maintain the status quo. When telling their own stories, unsuccessful students may be aware that they face barriers that realistically and inequitably restrict their opportunities for success, and yet they may still interpret their real and perceived failures as revealing something lacking in their character (Newman 1988).

For students of color and students of poverty, identification with the meritocratic master narrative as common sense creates a gulf between what they are told about access and opportunity for successful outcomes and the reality of their contexts. As Carter (2008) argues, the myth requires that students of color accept that racism, a structural barrier, is nonexistent, or at least does not function to curtail access and opportunity in schools. In this way, the repetition of meritocratic stories promotes a false equivalency that their hard work affords them similar, if not the same, outcomes as more privileged White, middle-class, students attending well-resourced suburban schools. This false equivalency further reifies and sustains the cultural value of the merit narrative as it is repeatedly normalized in policy, internalized by individuals in the context, and reproduced over and over again even in communities and schools most negatively impacted by the narrative (Sandlin & Clark 2009).

On the other hand, the master narrative is seemingly designed for White, middle-class, suburban students. We might even expect success to act as a reinforcer of meritocratic values for such high achievers, but, in fact, they do not seem well served either. For example, Luttrell cautions that privileged students may still exhibit fear of failing, a sense of "anxiety about losing their (unearned) advantages" (2008, 61). They may perceive success to be a fluke or a mistake or even a successful misrepresentation as they "fake it until they make it." To the degree to which they believe in the values of hard work and perseverance, they may doubt they are working hard enough and worry about being found out.

These negative implications occur because of the cyclical nature of the narrative: hard work and perseverance result in academic success. Academic success is the proof that one worked hard enough. Any setback indicates a lack of effort and a failure to persevere. Students learn they "failed on their own terms" (Liu 2011, 384). In addition, there is always another challenge on the horizon to strive toward. There can be no celebration of success or even rest following great effort because someone else somewhere else is still working. As American adults engage in a financial rat race, so do their youth in schools.

In part, we argue these negative implications result from the "generative" nature of redemptive self-stories (McAdams 2006). In so tightly focusing on continual growth and progress, success is only achievable when looking back in middle or late life. Yet, we present these same stories to youth as if they are able to look back at a lifetime of achievements and failures to see an overall pattern of success. McAdams (2006) argues that from the perspective of midlife, individuals come to understand that their failures have taught valuable lessons. We question whether the same is true for youth whose journey line stories cover a much shorter time frame and who likely have not yet achieved a "redemptive self" identity (nor is it developmentally appropriate for them to do so).

Thus, for both successful and unsuccessful students, we argue that this system functions to maintain minimum competency as the status quo. Successful students become averse to taking risks because they do not feel they have earned their current success and they fear failure. Unsuccessful students learn to blame themselves for their lack of success.

Further, because of the misidentification of norms for success and the hyper-individualized nature of the stories of success, merit narratives deemphasize structural and systemic barriers and fail to support advancement of marginalized and disenfranchised people. The normative nature of the meritocratic master narrative is why Kumashiro (2008) describes intentional work to address structural and institutional barriers as going against "common sense" in education. Going against common sense suggests that educators need to assess whether the stories they tell address structural inequities or whether they maintain the status quo. Not surprisingly, telling stories that go against common sense is difficult in a system built on individual merit and individual success. Kumashiro writes,

> Attempts to improve schooling that defy "common sense" have been dismissed as biased or politically motivated, as a distraction from the real work of schools, as inappropriate for children, or simply as nonsensical, particularly when the reforms call attention to such hot-button controversial issues as racism, sexism, poverty, and the ways that schools can reinforce them. (2008, 5)

As demonstrated in chapter 2, we argue it is also very difficult for educators to tell stories that defy what is perceived to be common sense and best practice for supporting underprivileged youth. The meritocratic master narrative is so entrenched that it is at the center of the stories educators tell about education, even when they are aware of the barriers their students face and even when asked about moments of personal courage that shape their equity and advocacy work in schools.

Kumashiro suggests that the entrenchment of merit narratives as good, even courageous, stories is a by-product of repetition. He writes:

> Students, educators, and researches, including those committed to social justice, often want certain forms of social change but resist others, sometimes knowingly, sometimes not. One reason that a desire for social change can coincide with a resistance to social change is that some educational practices, perspectives, social relations, and identities remain unquestioned. In fact, people often consider some practices and relations to be a part of what schools and society are supposed to be, and fail to recognize how repetition of such practices and relations—how having to experience them again and again—can help to maintain the oppressive status quo of schools and society. (Kumashiro 2000, 68)

Kumashiro's concerns with repetition are clear in chapter 2. The educators we interviewed found merit narratives to be so salient and persuasive that in reviewing their personal histories they mostly failed to tell stories that questioned or challenged inequities in their lives or the lives of their students. By overwhelmingly telling stories that center the values of hard work and perseverance, these educators may unintentionally reinforce existing social systems without highlighting how inequitable social structures impact the lives of their students.

CONTEXT OF THE STORYTELLING

We have presented educator stories that support the claim that when well-intentioned teachers tell success stories, they may also reinforce dominant metaphors of meritocracy (hard work and perseverance) as common-sense strategies in school settings that are exceptionally challenging. As Liu (2011) argued, these metaphors have the potential to impact the schools' meritocratic traditions, rituals, practices, processes, and procedures, but they also have the potential to impact students' understandings of themselves should they take up merit narratives and the metaphors of hard work and perseverance as identity markers (McAdams, 2006). In this chapter, we explore how student stories were consistent and inconsistent with the stories their educators told, especially as relates to (a) meritocracy and (b) courage.

The Students

We share here the stories of eight high school students, six juniors and two seniors. These students worked with the educators described in chapter 2. Half of the participants identified as cisgendered women and half identified as cisgendered men. The majority were students of color. Six identified as African Americans, one identified as an immigrant, and one identified White.

As a reminder, these students' schools were located in an area once known for industry and middle-class neighborhoods. Now, these schools are "urban-like" with high rates of enrollment of students of color and students of poverty. Milner's (2008) cautions about labels remain in effect, and it should be noted that these students recognized themselves and their peers as "at risk" and "underprivileged."

In addition, the students whose stories are presented here were chosen by their school counselor and an AP history teacher to be in a program designed to increase the number of African American students in advanced placements classes. The program originated because school leadership recognized that a sizable number of African Americans at the high school were eligible for AP classes yet were not guided to enroll in them. At the time, 54 percent of the students in the high school were African American, yet African Americans only made up 13 percent of students enrolled in AP courses. The school used the program to inform parents about AP opportunities and the benefits for their students if they took the courses. Program leaders held meetings in the community and provided after school support for the students who decided to enroll in advanced placement courses. The program lasted two years and served nearly twenty students over two years.

Storytelling: Journey Lines and Interviews

The storytelling process we used with students mirrored the process we used to collect stories from their educators. Like the educators, the students first completed a journey line of courage. As with the adults, the goal of the journey line was to surface important stories in the youths' lives and to act as an entry point to support students in connecting important stories to develop personal narratives. The journey line was followed by semi-structured interviews to explore the students' reflection and insight how and why they saw themselves as courageous in school. In engaging with journey line methodology, we were seeking to better understand stories that support or impede courageous orientations to schooling and learning.

ANALYSIS

As with the adult educators, interviews were audio recorded, transcribed, and de-identified prior to coding. Transcripts were analyzed holistically as stories and narratives rather than by response to interview questions and prompt. The analysis used a phenomenological approach to understand how students "take up" merit narratives told by their teachers as a matter of context and perspective (Heideggar 1962; Smith, Flowers, & Larkin 2009).

Transcripts were first analyzed holistically for three priori themes consistent with those shared by their educators. In particular, we were interested to the degree that students reiterated two heavily reported themes of the meritocratic master narrative. The first meritocratic theme included educator messages that students should work hard(er) and persevere because effort will have great rewards. The second meritocratic theme was alignment between success and courage. Specifically, we wanted to explore whether youth described courage in schools in the same way as adults did (i.e., by working harder and going beyond the expectations placed on their peers). The third theme was more systemic and structural in nature. We were interested in the degree to which students heard and took up advice that they should advocate for themselves in ways that effectively navigate school systems and structures.

Finally, consistent with Glaser and Strauss (1967), we allowed additional themes and categories also to arise as we worked through the students' responses so that we could examine the elements of student stories that were inconsistent or unique from their educator stories. As thematic codes arose, emergent descriptions were again recorded along with examples. The developing codebook was then subjected to peer debriefing (Marshall & Rossman 2006). Once theme descriptions were finalized, transcripts were independently coded. All coding disagreements were resolved in discussions between the researchers.

Themes

The following three themes arose from the students' shared stories. Like their educators, the students overwhelmingly shared stories consistent with the master narrative of meritocracy. In the first theme, there is no doubt that they took up the values of hard work and perseverance. Furthermore, they explicitly linked hard work, perseverance, going beyond expectations, and success with being courageous.

We argue that the second theme demonstrates the burden placed upon these youth through the repetition of the meritocratic master narrative in their lives. Specifically, in going beyond expectations, the youth were identified as role models and made, in part, responsible for the success of others. We argue that unlike the educators' generativity in giving back to the next generation, meritocratic self-stories positioned youth to think of themselves as different, and perhaps better than, their peers. Thus, another aspect of the hyper-individualizing meritocratic master narrative may lie in the idea that success leads to social isolation and increased responsibility. Even more concerning is that the youth saw taking on the cost of social isolation as a courageous act in service of establishing identity.

In the final theme, the degree to which educator messages about self- and collective advocacy were taken up is explored. Overall, students made few connections to advocacy in their own lives and contexts. In the very few examples provided, we found that courageous advocacy was more likely to be framed as an additional opportunity to demonstrate individual hard work and perseverance than as a strategic and collective story of navigation in local structures and systems.

Hard Work and Perseverance: "doing the best you can" (Cisgender Immigrant Man)

When asked about moments they recalled being courageous, students clearly espoused messages about the meritocratic values of hard work and perseverance. All eight interviews were coded as having these themes, and all eight students self-identified as hard workers. Further analysis of the excerpts coded as hard work and perseverance revealed the following findings.

First, consistent with the meritocratic master narrative, students saw hard work as a temporary sacrifice for long-term success. As one student summarized, "Well, I dedicate most of my free time to schoolwork. I don't really do anything else, because I know that should come first" (Cisgender African American Woman). After carefully outlining his study habits, one student concluded with, " . . . and that's why I work so hard in school because I want to reach that level" (Cisgender White Man). As another student explained, "I didn't want to take Spanish, or something like a language, but then I'm glad that I did, because even now, even though it's hard, it's worth it" (Cisgender African American Woman). Across the interviews, this idea that their efforts were "worth it" because they would be awarded with success later, after schooling, was clear in all students' stories. While the students rarely used the phrase "American Dream," they were counting on abstracted attainment of a "good life" in the future because of the sacrifices they were making as students.

Second, students described their hard work in competitive terms. For example, in recalling her choice to take AP coursework, one student laughingly complained, "Everybody hyped it up like it was going to be fun and stuff, but really I had to study for the first time . . . Now I actually have to study in order to keep up" (Cisgender African American Woman). The need to not only keep up but get ahead was emphasized across interviews. For example, one student described, "taking, like, the AP classes and the harder classes," as a competitive advantage because, "you get that step on other people" (Cisgender African American Man). Thus, students felt hard work was "worth it" because of the competitive advantage it would give them both in school and after school. This language is again consistent with the American meritocratic master narrative and the US competitive capitalist market.

Third, students explicitly identified their hard work as a courageous act. For example, one student explained how what might look like compliant behavior is actually courageous behavior.

> I take care of anything the teachers ask me or my parents ask me or any adult asks me. So, it really shows up as doing the best you can in school. That's basically showing that you are caring for your assignment or whatever your mother or teacher or your parents have asked you to do. That's courage in its own sense. (Cisgender Immigrant Man)

Hard work was courageous work in part because *doing the best you can* is the same as *going beyond expectations* (i.e., what was expected for students in their school contexts). For example, one student told us, "I guess for me it's doing the whole AP thing because that's what people consider courageous because they know that it's going to be harder than a normal class" (Cisgender African American Woman). Note here that these students self-identified as courageous, but also believed others, both peers and adults, would see their hard work as courageous acts. A very similar explanation was given by another student:

> I would say I was courageous in my grades, in like getting all As, and my attendance, and everything because a lot of people don't do that. A lot of people don't care about school. I mean, yeah, they don't. So, I feel like I'm among the few that really do care about education and that really do take their school work serious. (Cisgender African American Woman)

The alignment between the educators' descriptions of courage and their students' descriptions of courage is clear and consistent throughout. These students identified as courageous because their hard work set them apart from their peers and identified them as willing and able to go beyond expectations. There is a troubling implication here, however, in that these youth believed that academic success was not an expectation for students in their context. In fact, they believed that most adults in their lives expected minimum competency from students. Additional ways in which these students distinguished themselves from the norm and from expectations in their context is further explored in the next section.

Fourth, while hard work was clear in how the students described coursework, perseverance was more often described in their stories about athletics. For example, one student described her choice to participate in a school sport as, "I was horrible at it, but I was learning, and I remember, I want to really practice at this so that I can get better 'cause I actually like the sport" (Cisgender African American Woman). Given these students were already relatively high performing when chosen to participate in the AP program, one explanation for the prevalence of perseverance stories in the context of athletics could be that athletics offered more opportunity to demonstrate effort to overcome obstacles.

However, one African American young man and one White young man were selected for school teams (i.e., identified as having athletic talent). In both cases, they shared stories of how their perseverance, despite physical limitations, was courageous. For example, the African American student recalled how he felt when joining the varsity team as a freshman, stating, "I was scared . . . and the kids were just a lot bigger than me, a lot of seniors. So that was intimidating, but I stuck with it" (Cisgender African American Man). The White student felt similarly about trying to find his role on the team following an injury. In both cases, their motivation to persevere was based in what they felt they owed their teammates. As the young man recovering from injury summarized,

> I still felt like I had to be a part of the team. And I owed a lot of my teammates, because, being a leader, being a quarterback, I thought that was an important thing to be with the team. So I decided the next year that I was going to be a kicker. So I would just kick and so I would avoid all of that potential injury and still be a part of the team and help out in whatever way possible. So I felt that was something courageous that I took on, because I could have just given up and supported them in some other way, but I still wanted to be there as a member. (Cisgender White Man)

Interestingly, given the educator stories provided in the previous chapter, none of the students indicated they learned the values of hard work and perseverance from the stories their teachers told. In fact, the youth did not repeat any of the "success" stories their educators reported they shared with students. Instead, they mostly pointed to the mentorship within their families. For example, one student explained, "My parents always told me always keep trying, just really never give up, just from their teachings influence me to do things like this now" (Cisgender African American Woman). Another student shared the pride he takes in his family's hard work. He said:

> Our family is hardworking. I would say because my dad, he works until 8:00 and he goes to work about 6:00 in the morning and comes back at 8:00 and not only . . . You know how usually on weekends, you just, like, chill on a weekend? He doesn't do that. (Cisgender Immigrant Man)

In fact, only one student shared a story about mentorship outside the family. He stated, "Like pastors in my church and just people on the street, they see me and they, like, care about what I do in school and sports. And they pull me aside and they talk to me about it" (Cisgender African American Man). Thus, there is a good deal of alignment between educator and student stories, but the students identify these themes as coming from their family and community instead of the school. This supports the argument that the meritocratic master narrative operates on a cultural level, even as it is enacted in school systems.

Nonetheless, it is clear from the stories the youth told indicate they explicitly took up the themes of hard work and perseverance. They accepted a central tenet of meritocracy that their hard work would result in future success. They identified stories in which perseverance was necessary, but, unlike the educators, they distinguished between hard work and perseverance. Hard work was more often associated with academics and their individual success, whereas perseverance was more often associated with athletics and the team's success. Moreover, within the school context, students explicitly took up hard work as courageously going beyond the expectations adults have of youth in this context.

Responsibility and Isolation: "I felt the need to stick up" (Cisgender African American Woman)

The demonstration of hard work and perseverance in school contexts led the youth to be identified as role models for younger siblings and peers. One student described her modeling as "bringing others into their success" (Cisgender African American Woman). This idea that demonstration of one's hard work and perseverance made one responsible for fostering the same in others was consistent throughout the stories, but the degree to which identification as a role model was perceived as problematic differed across academic and athletic contexts.

For the most part, the youth were proud to describe the positive influence of their athletic accomplishments on younger siblings. The following two examples demonstrate how the youth positively described modeling athletic accomplishments for siblings.

> I mean, I think my little brother looks up to me a lot more, so I guess seeing me. I know he went to see me swim a lot. I think that he might actually be inspired to do something like that, to play sports. (Cisgender African American Woman)

> I'll say they see what I'm doing and they're like, "Oh, that's good, so I want to do it too!" Like my little sister, she sees me do cheering, she'll try to imitate the cheers and stuff, and she says she wants to do cheer too now. (Cisgender African American Woman)

However, descriptions of acting as an academic role model were much more ambivalent. The burden of responsibility was especially clear when students described how they needed to be role models for siblings in academic contexts. For example, one student described his relationship with his siblings, "they look up to me and they see something that they want to be whenever they get older. So I try and carry myself in a way that they will look up to and respect" (Cisgender White Man).

Similarly, many of the shared stories suggested the students experienced additional tension in their family relationships when they were asked to model academic merit. For example, one student described tensions that arose when her parents, "they, like, reward me and stuff like that. And then they try to get my siblings to do good because they see that I'm doing good" (Cisgender African American Woman).

The ambivalence about role modeling was most clear in the stories told by the one White student:

> I feel like it drives her to be more like me. I feel like I'm a good role model for her, although it's kind of difficult. I feel bad for her sometimes because a lot of times my parents are, like, so proud of me that if she doesn't do as well, she feels bad about herself that she may not do as well. So I always try to be positive with her and help her with things. So in that sense it's a difficulty for me, but I also think that it's a good progressive thing for me to help her out, and feel empathy, and just be able to be a positive role model and help her continue. (Cisgender White Man)

Given these descriptions, we worry that role modeling introduced tensions in sibling relationships.

Such tensions were further indicated in peer relationships when the students positioned themselves as knowing more or better than their friends. For example, one student shared a story about trying to act as a role model for a friend:

I try to because, like, she had an incident. And she made a bad choice. And I tried to get her to make a good choice. Like saying, "Oh, I'm not supporting this." And she still made the bad choice. Like I tried to get them to do good. Even if they don't listen, I still, like, keep telling them and telling them, like, "You're not going to end up anywhere if you going to keep making these bad choices." (Cisgender African American Woman)

In this example, the student implies that she is the kind of person who is "going" places, and at the same time, that her friend is not going to be that kind of person unless she can make better choices. This contrasting between herself and her friends is clear in a later story where she describes her friends, "they get into a lot of drama, so I'm not getting into all of that. You shouldn't, because it's not worth it" (Cisgender African American Woman). It is also interesting how explicitly hard work is cited as "worth it," but drama with friends is not.

The care these youth took to position themselves as different, and often better, than their peers was common throughout their stories. For example, one student discussed the ways he acted as a role model to his peers, stating, "Well I make straight As, so that's giving them something to look to as well, something that they are going to follow. And I try to help them in school." His explanation of his modeling continued with an explicit discussion of how he differs from his peers: "I stay away from drugs and everything. Like how all the kids they go off and party and stuff while I stay at home and do schoolwork and work on my athletics" (Cisgender African American Man). "All the kids" and "the crowd" were common phrases this student used to differentiate his own position from that of his peers. For example, he reported:

> It's so easy to get pulled in with the crowd, so I think staying away from the crowd and doing your own little thing, I think that shows courage. Just like how they party all the time. It's like a bunch of parties all the time over the weekend. And like, not too long ago, they had [inaudible] and stuff and everybody went to that. And I thought that it was pretty courageous to stay home and didn't go to that.

A very similar message was conveyed by his teammate, who told us:

> So in my free time, where some people may just go out and do things, I like to read things. I like to look at my chemistry book because I'm preparing for my AP exam. I do like doing things like that. Like I said, I consider myself to be a "lifelong learner." I feel that after college I'm still going to want to read textbooks because that's just something I'm interested in. So I feel like that's courageous for me to take on that challenge, rather than just going out with the crowd and going out to parties and whatever they are doing. I feel that's something courageous and I, just being dedicated to what I do, sports, school. (Cisgender White Man)

Note how these two different students referred to distancing themselves from their peers as courageous. This framing of separating self from peers as a courageous act was consistent in the stories of other students as well. For example, one student described a courageous act of "cutting off" a former friend, stating, "Like, I have this friend, she like, she's not a good influence. But I wouldn't say she's rubbing off on me. But I don't think she'll benefit me in any way, me being friends with her, so I've, like, kind of, basically, cut her off" (Cisgender African American Woman).

This idea of courage as separating or distinguishing oneself from the norm was further propagated in the stories the students told about their own courage and youth they identified as particularly courageous. Similar to the classic Erikson (1968) identity definition, courage for these students was fidelity to one's self independent from social relationships. For example, multiple students identified youth examples of "independent courage," where they cited how their peers were going against the norm and "finding their own path" (Cisgender Immigrant Man). They noted their courageous peers "don't have to follow the status quo or, like, be in one group or be followers" (Cisgender African American Woman). As one student put it, "I think they're representing, basically, their self. Like, it doesn't have anything to do with anybody else. Like they are, basically, saying, 'I don't care what you think,' whenever they do something like that" (Cisgender African American Woman).

One student described herself as courageous in this same way as the youth described others:

> I don't tend to follow the crowd as much as other people would and well I've never been like a follower, like never felt the need to really blend in with anybody because if you look at me, I cannot blend in with anybody! (Cisgender African American Woman)

But most students identified themselves as courageous when they voiced their opinions or "felt the need to stick up" (Cisgender African American Woman), without knowing how the group would react. For example, one student said she felt courageous, "speaking in front of others and you don't know how people are going to react. It's what you believe in" (Cisgender African American Woman). Similarly, another said, "Because I don't know how the other person is going to react. I don't want to seem 'fake,' as everybody says. To me, it's what I have to do. It doesn't matter what they think" (Cisgender African American Woman).

It is clear throughout this theme that there are burdens in taking up the meritocratic master narrative as youth. These students' demonstration of hard work, perseverance, and success resulted in their identification as role models for siblings and peers. There was evidence that this positioning led to tensions in both family and peer relationships, but one of the striking aspects was the degree to which the youths' stories served to distinguish themselves from peers who fail to work as hard as they do.

This separation and isolation was further demonstrated in the students' description of courage as not following or caring about "the crowd."

Advocacy Without Navigation

Students clearly took up messages about the importance of advocacy. However, unlike the messages their educators' stories communicated about the importance of self-advocacy, the focus of the students' advocacy efforts was primarily at the level of larger social and political issues. For example, students identified issues that inspired their advocacy efforts including, Black Lives Matter (Cisgender African American Woman), LGBTQIA rights (Cisgender African American Women), and racist federal policies (Cisgender African American Woman).

There was little evidence that the students picked up navigation or saw the importance of strategy in working within the systems and structures of their personal and local context. Despite the educators' efforts to support students to advocate for themselves, only two students took up local community issues and only one student took up an issue related to the school. For example, one student explained an issue that he was inspired by, "Just violence 'cause we have a lot of violence in this community and people are trying to step up and change that" (Cisgender African American Man). In this case, the student was not personally involved in advocacy efforts, but explained this was a place in which courage for local advocacy was needed.

In another case, a student was identified by several peers as a source of courage because she was trying to restart a community newspaper. Both the peers and the student herself explained she was courageous because of the extra work she was taking on without support, rather than because of any community advocacy. Thus, this example seems to better fit the themes of hard work and perseverance than of advocacy and navigation.

Finally, one student shared a story about trying to advocate for changes within the school system. She explained,

> Black History Month and we never spoke about Black history at all. I don't even know why. I was so astonished. We talked about Christopher Columbus and we talked about all the relations. We talked about Buddhism, Muslims. And we talked about everything except Black history. I asked him, "What was that?" And he said, "In the curriculum, there's really no space for that." I don't understand how, I guess. He said, "In the curriculum, they don't really go over it. And they don't really review it because they'd done so much other things and try and teach you so many other things that they don't have time for that." And I was confused, because, I mean, it's Black History, why wouldn't you talk about that, right? (Cisgender African American Woman)

As shared by this student, the issue was identified, but advocacy efforts did not move forward. This is a great example of the types of problems the educators wanted to help students navigate, but in this case, navigation failed. The student was unable to communicate the issue in a way that pushed forward change with the curriculum.

Like with the adults, the structural and systemic stories of collective advocacy were missing or minimized behind the individual stories of hard work. There was some evidence that students aligned themselves with important social issues that are part of a national conversation. However, the connections between the larger national conversation and their own lives was abstracted for most students. In contrast to what their educators hoped for them, these students did not make connections to advocacy in their own lives and contexts. Instead, the most courageous example was reframed as a choice to engage in additional, not required, hard work, alone and without support from peers or adults.

DOES TIMING MATTER?

We learned several important things from this exploration of educator and student stories. These shared stories suggest that, like educators, students do not appear to break out of the meritocratic master narratives, even when one might argue that these narratives do not serve them well. Both youth and adults identify going beyond expectations and working hard(er) than peers as a courageous act.

However, in contrast to the stories adult educators told, youth narratives are forward looking. It is clear here that students have taken up the values of hard work and perseverance, believing it is "worth it" because doing so will lead to future success. Students seemingly embrace a "prove them wrong" attitude that supports their hard work in the face of low expectations (Bergin & Cooks 2002; Grantham & Ford 2003; Mehan, Hubbard, & Villanueva 1994), but we question whether this is an adaptive strategy in the end. The way these youth (re)tell meritocratic themes differs from the way adults told stories of achieving success and tied those stories back to the master narrative. We wonder if the lack of perspective (i.e., evidence of a pattern of success) means there are greater burdens placed on youth than on adults when taking up the meritocratic master narrative. We know from their stories that youth were positioned as role models, made responsible for the success of their peers, and that they were self-identified as different or better than peers who fail to work as hard as they do.

This hyper-individualizing nature of the meritocratic master narrative troubles us, particularly when these stories are retold and reimagined by students of color. For example, we know from the critical race theory literature that connection to the Black community provides a sense of meaning and purpose for students as well as a positive academic identity necessary for school achievement (e.g., Carter 2008; Oyersman, Gant, & Ager 1995). Likewise, Perry, Steele, and Hilliard (2003) argue that for African American students to achieve, they need to be grounded in their identity as part of a racial group so that are able to interpret and make sense of the structural barriers associated with racism and discrimination they face in schools. We worry that meritocratic cultural narrative renders these systemic effects invisible as youth individualize and take up burdens that are not their own in an effort to utilize the commonsense strategies causally linked to future success in meritocratic school stories.

Thus, we turn now to questioning how we might disrupt such pervasive common-sense stories. We aspire to produce educators who transform the stories they tell about academic success into communal stories that do not leave students feeling isolated and weighed down by the responsibilities placed on them by inequitable systems. In the next chapter, we will examine case studies and question how we might retell stories to be more effective.

FOUR
Reframing the Stories We Tell

We began this book by sharing how our stories brought us together. The process of sharing our stories and finding the commonalities within them lead us to deeper and more in-depth discussions about our individual schooling and professional experiences. Stories of hard work and perseverance got us through school, K–12, and graduate programs, but failed to provide a way forward that did not require us to individually carry the burden put upon us by an inequitable educational system. The data from our work demonstrates that the same stories are being told to students by well-meaning and self-professed advocates for educational change. This understanding suggests that we must challenge these stories because they do not create access and opportunity for students in today's schools and in their future professional lives. In other words, while we survived our educational systems, we know that more students like us will not survive unless we tell systemic stories that focus on changing the inequities that students face in schools. To be clear, we do not want to lose the stories that we were told, we want to reframe them from *individual stories of success* to *collective stories of success*. In doing so, we believe that students will not have to choose between school success and their communities nor will they be as isolated.

This chapter is our attempt to consciously and intentionally tell different stories by first, raising awareness about the stories we tell and retell in our heads and second, learning how to tell different stories, stories that collectively support student success without exacerbating the burdens that youth and their families experience within inequitable educational systems.

THE COLLECTIVE STORY

To create a collective story, we have to intentionally tell stories that resonate "with the stories a community already holds in mind, particularly with the public narratives—religious, historical, ideological and popular—that are at the core of a community's culture" (Mayer 2014, 102). Our data suggest that while the meritocracy narrative is elevated as the narrative of the United States, it does not hold true for the historical and popular narratives that many underserved and under-resourced students hold in their minds. In our opinion, the meritocracy narrative is forced upon students (and their families) in ways that create tensions between home and school. As educators, we ask: How might we get teachers to challenge the prevailing narrative by constructing a narrative that better serves the interest of their students? To help us understand how to do this, we turn to Mayer's (2014) work on narratives in politics. He writes,

> More importantly, certainly from the standpoint of collective action, narratives can construct our interests. Interests are typically taken as given by social scientists. Yet, even interests based on fundamental egoistic desires for security, power, or wealth may be partially constructed. And clearly our non-egoistic interests—in the fate of others we care about, in causes that move us, or in the fortunes of the community of which we are a member—are largely constructed. Narratives can play a role in each case. (2014, 87)

Our desire to provide an alternative narrative to the meritocracy narrative is centered within constructing (and ultimately supporting) non-egoistic interests. We believe that if teachers intentionally built narratives rooted "in the fate of others we care about, in causes that move us, or in the fortunes of the community of which we are a member" (Mayer 2014, 87), then the stories that they construct would not force students to choose between community and school nor would students believe that in order to be successful that they must take up hyper-individualism as the story of success. As teacher educators, our hope lies in our ability to teach pre-service and in-service teachers how to construct different stories. Yet, Mayer reminds us that hope and good intentions will not lead us to different stories. Instead, we must be knowledgeable about how to craft new stories and to ensure that they are rooted in the culture of the youth being served. He continues,

> To assert that narrative *can* construct such interests, however, does not predict when it will. For that reason I explore the question of what factors affect when a story will be taken up by a community, acknowledging that the efficacy of a story depends in part on the alignment with material interests and in part on who has access to the megaphone, but also arguing that the power of the story depends on the skill of the storyteller in telling a story that resonates with the stories a

community already has in mind, with the narratives of the culture. (Mayer 2014, 103)

Below we offer cases modeled on our experiences in schools as teacher educators and scholars. We ask you to think through how we might re-create, reimagine, and recast these very typical educational stories that represent the everyday experiences of educators and students in school systems so that they resonate with the stories that underserved and under-resourced communities already tell.

CASE #1—WHAT ABOUT ME?

DeVante is a quiet observant tenth grader. He is the middle of three children in his family. His older brother is in the twelfth grade and plays football. DeVante's brother is popular with his peers as evidenced by the fact that all the students in the building know him. DeVante's younger sister is in the ninth grade and gets good grades. It is clear to DeVante that his sister is popular with teachers. Because the building is so small, he is often compared to his brother and sister. DeVante has come to understand that he is just DeVante. That he does not possess any special gifts or talents, except his love of all things comics and his ability to draw them. Unfortunately, this special talent often gets DeVante in trouble because he is viewed as a daydreamer that is not putting forth his best effort.

While DeVante is often overlooked or dismissed in the building, this is not the case in Mr. Taylor's class. Mr. Taylor teaches Graphic Design II, III, and IV. This is the first time that DeVante has had Mr. Taylor and it is the first time that he feels "good about himself" in school. In this class, DeVante is able to be himself while demonstrating his ability to design compelling visual graphics for websites and social media. DeVante does not daydream in Mr. Taylor's class because time flies when he is there. It is an elective which means that it is only one semester instead of two like an academic course. Because it is a popular elective, it is filled to capacity which means that not everyone gets to work on a computer every class meeting. Despite this, DeVante still looks forward to the class and is often annoyed when the class is over.

The school year is coming to an end and DeVante finds himself in the guidance office selecting his courses for next year. Mrs. Hill has been a guidance counselor at the school for twenty-five years and is counting down to retirement. She is often amazed by how much the school has changed in twenty-five years and finds herself at a loss for how to best serve students who are not college-bound. There are barely jobs in the region for college graduates, let alone students who are not going to college. Ninety percent of the resources she has access to are for students who want to attend a four-year college or university and that is less than

40 percent of her student population. She became a counselor so that she could help students improve their station in life and to make the best choices while doing it. Yet, the past ten years have been challenging.

DeVante appears in her office to go over his schedule. Mrs. Hill has fifteen minutes with him because she has to see exactly one-half of the nine hundred students in the building. She tells DeVante that he has to take eleventh-grade algebra, eleventh-grade English, eleventh-grade US government, and eleventh-grade earth science. He gets to select two electives, one from in the health sciences and one in technology. The only thing that DeVante cares about is Graphic Design III, the next level class he could take with Mr. Taylor. Mrs. Hill checks the schedule and says, "I am sorry, that class does not fit your schedule. Because you need these particular academic courses, graphic design III is not an option for you." She goes on to tell DeVante that if he pushes himself and doubles up on either math or science in the eleventh grade, that he could take Graphic Design III and IV in the twelfth grade. This is possible, but will be challenging for him. He would have to "work really hard" next year. It is up to him, but is totally possible if he wants it bad enough. Mrs. Hill assures DeVante that she believes that he can do it, if he would just "give his best effort" like his sister does.

Questions

1. What educational story do you imagine is told about DeVante? What should he do? How should he do it?
2. What story do you think is told about Mr. Taylor? About Mrs. Hill?
3. Where in this case are people telling stories (or making judgments) about hard work, perseverance, and success?
4. What other assets (individual and within the community) beyond hard work and perseverance are evident?
5. Think of an educational story that you might tell if we enacted the resources identified in question 4 with a community lens instead of the individual story we see here.

CASE #2 — IS THIS THE BEST I CAN DO?

Tonya had been teaching math for eight years now and she is tired. Tired of the constant questioning by leadership about why she allowed kids with low standardized tests scores into her class. Tired of the constant nagging from her peers about the noise level in her classroom. "You could not possibly be teaching math with all that noise I heard in that room!" was the constant criticism. Tonya had become a math teacher so that she could expose Black children and poor children to math in a way that touched their lives and built upon their spirits. You see, Tonya

LOVED math and she wanted her students to love it as well. She had chosen to teach at Sparrow Middle School because it was in her old neighborhood and it was there that she began to genuinely love math. Her math teacher, Mrs. Harrison, made math fun and relatable. She knew in sixth grade that she wanted to be a teacher. But now, she is just tired.

She had gone to one of the best schools of education in the state and had passed the certification and basic skills exams on the first try. Tonya understood how difficult tests like these were for Black aspiring teachers like herself, so when she passed it she became a tutor to others. After teaching for three years, she had gone back to school to get her masters' degree because she wanted to stay on top of her game. She wanted to show her colleagues that she was good (she was the only Black teacher in the building) and she wanted to be the best for her students. Lord knows they deserved the best teachers, given how little else they were given.

While the school was great when she was a student, it had definitely gotten worse. Charter schools in the area had taken nearly a fifth of the student population by promising better academic outcomes for students, smaller class sizes, and committed teachers. The leadership was feeling the budget crunch and had hunkered down on standardized tests as the measure of excellence. Teacher (and student) accountability talk saturated every meeting. As a result, teachers were anxious, angry, and frustrated. They knew they were doing their best and yet the scores were not showing it. They had developed a tendency to talk about all student related matters as a lack of student effort and parental involvement. Tonya was exhausted.

Upon becoming a teacher, Tonya had promised herself that she would never let the system kill her joy for teaching. She understood how inequitable systems operate. They are perfectly designed to get the inequitable outcomes they produce. When one of her college professors said this in class, it was a light bulb moment for her. She would rise above the system and model for students the possibilities of using one's God given gifts for good. In her case, her God given gift in math would be used for the good of teaching young people math.

But, now she was just tired. Constant beratement by leadership, "Your scores are *still* low." Never mind that she was demonstrating significant student growth each year; it was not enough. Her students came to her already behind in every math competency. Even significant growth would not get them to where they needed to be. Unfortunately, her peers were the worst. She felt they hated her eternal optimism and viewed it as an indictment of what they were not doing. For this reason, they complained about every little thing she did, but most especially about the noise coming from her classroom.

While at a professional development program at a local university, Tonya met an administrator from a neighboring school district. She was looking for Black teachers in STEM and wanted to know if Tonya was interested in moving. This was a difficult choice for Tonya. After all, Sparrow Middle was her community and she had built a professional career on the premise that they needed her and that she would rise above the nonsense. But her heart was heavy. She went to the interview.

The promise of a new system lifted Tonya's spirit. She would be the lead teacher. She would have a little more freedom with the curriculum (not much, but some). More importantly, she would get a $15,000 raise. This was big for her. She took the job.

Two years into the lead teacher role in the new school district, Tonya has come full circle. Her team thinks she is doing the students a disservice by introducing concepts they can't possibly understand. They think that her expectation that they call parents monthly is above and beyond the Union's expectations, and they think that she is too young to actually know what she is doing. She arrives an hour early to work every day, but again finds herself tired. Teaching this way is just not sustainable.

Questions

1. What educational story do you imagine is told about Tonya? What story do you think is told about her school?
2. What story do you think is told about her students? About her colleagues?
3. Where in this case are people telling stories (or making judgments) about hard work, perseverance, and success?
4. What other assets (individual and within the community) beyond hard work and perseverance are evident?
5. Think of an educational story that you might tell if we enacted the resources identified in question 4 with a community lens instead of the individual story we see here.

CASE #3—BUT I'M AN ALLY...

Amanda has been teaching high school history for a couple of years at her dream job, a district much like she grew up in—suburban, upper middle class, and mostly White. She gets these kids. She was one of them.

Amanda always knew she wanted to be a teacher. Her mom was a teacher and so was an aunt, though they both taught elementary. She played school with her younger siblings and taught her dolls how to read.

Amanda initially thought she'd teach elementary school too, but her teacher education program opened her eyes. She learned about the importance of equity work in schools. She read about her "invisible knapsack" of White privilege (McIntosh 1988) and she vowed not to advance "the culture of power" in her classroom (Delpit 2006). She was inspired by her studies, switching to secondary history (even though it was much more difficult) and picking up additional courses in psychology and sociology as electives. She considers herself an ally and a social justice advocate for the young adults she teaches.

Although she is living the dream job, she had been initially disappointed that she would be teaching a relatively scripted curriculum designed to raise scores on the AP history exams. She had spoken with her principal about her undergraduate coursework and her ideas for revamping the curriculum so that the voices of people of color, women, and the poor would be heard in the readings. Her principal told her that he couldn't, in good conscience, alter a curriculum that was working so well for student pass rates on the AP exams. Of course, she understood . . . but still . . .

Then the principal pulled her aside after a staff meeting. There had been some student civility issues of late. "Kids being kids" and just "mouthing the words they heard on the news," but parents were concerned. Would she consider teaching an elective about "race, ethnicity, gender, and so on"? Amanda leapt at the chance.

Amanda was ready and willing to put in the work! She reviewed all her undergraduate readings. She wrote the syllabus and prepped for the new class. Advisors recommended their high-performing, college-bound students for the course. The principal and counselors started talking about the course as preparing kids for college, making them more aware of people they may meet when they ventured outside the lack of the diversity in their school district.

But it's not as easy as she thought. The kids don't seem to be worried about their invisible backpacks and they don't seem to be inspired in the ways she was. Today, she was trying to have a civil debate about immigration and current US policy. She knew that the students had worked very hard on their internet research to prepare. At the beginning of class, she reminded everyone about civility and to be nice to their peers, even if they disagree on the politics. Fifteen minutes in, and half the room was talking about "kids in cages" and the other half were using language like, "Build the wall." She tried to make sure everyone's voice was heard and respected, but she had to admit she hadn't gotten to an effective stopping place when the bell rang.

Even though she did her best, she's worried it's not good enough. What makes it worse is that her principal now wants to meet. Some parents have complained about "politics" in her classroom and have concerns about her classroom management.

Questions

1. What educational story do you imagine is told about Amanda? What should she do? How should she do it?
2. What story do you think is told about her students? About her school? About the rigor of her teaching philosophy?
3. Where in this case are people telling stories (or making judgments) about hard work, perseverance, and success?
4. What other assets (individual and within the community) beyond hard work and perseverance are evident?
5. Think of an educational story that you might tell if we enacted the resources identified in question 4 with a community lens instead of the individual story we see here.

CASE #4—FAKING IT UNTIL YOU
MAKE IT . . . I WILL MAKE IT, RIGHT?

Katlyn attends a magnet school that focuses on STEM education. Her parents chose it because the math and science focus would put her on "the right path" for college (hopefully, pre-med). She is in the running for valedictorian next year. Her GPA is maybe the highest, or at least in the top three, depending on how P.E. grades are calculated this term and how well her last biology exam went. She's already taken the SAT and ACT and done well above the cut points for her target colleges ("good state schools," but not Ivys), but she still has time to take them again and improve her scores.

And she knows that it's important to show you can do more than academic work. She runs track, plays cello, and volunteers reading to preschoolers at the local library. She's made an appointment with the guidance counselor to talk about other volunteer or internship opportunities. She thinks it would be good if she could find something helping the poor or maybe working with minority students in the city. Something to show she understands and cares about the big issues.

The day of the appointment with her guidance counselor is a rough day. She got back that biology test and it was barely an A. She's going to have to ask for extra credit if she wants to stay competitive for valedictorian. She was up late studying for civics. She's feeling tired and kind of down. When Mr. Williams asks what's wrong (Where's your smile today?), she takes a breath and quietly asks, "What if I don't get into college?" Mr. Williams, sighs and rubs his eyes, "This again? You're such a smart girl. Why do you keep worrying?" The quietness in Katlyn's voice is gone, anxiety clear in her tone: "I'm really *not that* smart. I just work hard. And I'll be competing with all those other kids who are actually smart!" Mr. Williams sighs again. "Katlyn, all those kids feel just like you.

You just got to do what they do. Keep on working. You just got to keep on going. When all else fails, fake it until you make it. You're going to be fine."

Questions

1. What educational story do you imagine is told about Katlyn? What should she do? How should she do it? What educational story do you imagine Katlyn tells about herself?
2. What story do you think is told about Mr. Williams? About other kids like Katlyn?
3. Where in this case are people telling stories (or making judgments) about hard work, perseverance, and success?
4. What other assets (individual and within the community) beyond hard work and perseverance are evident?
5. Think of an educational story that you might tell if we enacted the resources identified in question 4 with a community lens instead of the individual story we see here.

CASE #5—WHAT SHOULD I DO?

Jim teaches secondary English at a school struggling to define itself in the wake of redistricting. The school used to serve a mix of white- and blue-collar families, primarily from the White neighborhood in which the school is located. Now the population is getting more racially diverse. Jim doesn't worry about it. Kids are kids and they all need to learn English.

The pacing guide says this month is all about rhetorical analysis. It's also Black History month and Jim thinks "Two birds, one stone." He's teaching rhetoric using Dr. Martin Luther King Jr.'s sermons. He figures the kids already know about the "I Have a Dream" speech. He knows it was studied in history to honor MLK Jr day last month. He figures that even though this is the first time he's used these sermon texts, the students have already had discussions about the Civil Rights Movement in US history and are ready for this lesson.

He brings in audio recordings of the sermon and asks the students to read along with a transcript. As the congregation shouts out during the speech, the students first start to giggle and then by the end, they're laughing every time it happens. Jim warns the class that they need to pay attention in order to identify key passages for the analysis. Afterwards, he wonders how successful the audio was. Should he have stuck with the transcripts?

At the end of the unit, Jim asks the students to write a rhetorical analysis of a modern civil rights source. The students will also briefly present their analysis to the class. He reminds students that the text is up to them, but that they should censor any "sensitive" language that might offend their peers.

Students submit their essays for feedback before planning their presentation. Jim understands about bias, so he sets the website the class uses to turn in papers (and that allows him to run them through TurnItIn.com) to grade blindly. There's clearly a mix of texts and opinions in the class, with some students thinking that racism has improved and others thinking it has gotten worse. One of the essays has a note at the bottom: "I know what you're trying to do here. But not much of this will change anything anyway. I can't wait to graduate and get away from these MAGAts once and for all." He takes a minute to think before he identifies which student wrote the paper. What should he do?

Questions

1. What educational story do you imagine is told about Jim's students? What should he do? How should he do it?
2. What story do you think is told about Jim's teaching philosophy? About his beliefs about his students?
3. Where in this case are people telling stories (or making judgments) about hard work, perseverance, and success?
4. What other assets (individual and within the community) beyond hard work and perseverance are evident?
5. Think of an educational story that you might tell if we enacted the resources identified in question 4 with a community lens instead of the individual story we see here.

CASE #6—IS THE PANDEMIC REALLY THAT AWFUL? (CASE STUDY BY RAMONA CRAWFORD)

Michael is a charismatic and athletic fourteen-year-old. He is the second youngest of four children but the only boy in his family. His mother is a single parent and typically works two jobs but was laid off from one due to the COVID-19 pandemic. She still works from 8:00 a.m.–4:00 p.m. daily but relies on public transportation to get around so her commute, which typically starts at 6:30 a.m. and ends at 5:30 p.m. Consequently, the kids are responsible for themselves before and after school with the two older sisters taking on the majority of the responsibilities.

Prior to the students engaging in virtual learning due to the COVID-19 pandemic, his two older sisters attended classes in person at the local high school while his younger sister attended the elementary school in the same district. Although Michael is fourteen, he attends the middle school in the area because he was left behind in the seventh grade due to his poor attendance and failing grades. Although he is behind academically, he is a three sport athlete and the star player on his school's football team. The teachers in his school recognize his athletic potential but none of them have been successful at keeping him out of trouble and on grade level academically. Michael frequently displays maladaptive behaviors and gets into verbal altercations with the teachers due to his boisterous personality.

In the beginning of the Fall 2020 school year, the students in the district were attending classes virtually. After many failed virtual school attempts, due to technical difficulties and low student engagement, the district decided to have the parents vote on if they wanted their children to attend school in person, online only, or in a hybrid format where students attended school in person two days a week and engaged in virtual learning two days a week. Michael's mom voted to send all of her kids to school in person full-time so that she could continue to work her 8:00 a.m.–4:00 p.m. shift while also looking for another job to work overnight.

This is the third week of in-person classes and Ms. Graham, the supervisor at the neighborhood recreation center, notices Michael playing basketball alone during school hours. She engages in several conversations with him about not being in school during hours of operation, but Michael insists that he is taking classes virtually this week and is on a lunch break when Ms. Graham sees him. After the third encounter, Ms. Graham decides to call his mom to check in on the situation. Michael's mother informs Ms. Graham that she only knows about one missed day but assures her that she will stay on top of him in the future.

The following week, as Ms. Graham is driving to the community recreation center, she sees Michael playing outside with a group of friends. She pulls over to talk to all of the neighborhood kids to ask them how school is going amid the coronavirus pandemic and asks about their grades. Noticing that Michael is silent throughout the conversation, she pulls him to the side for a one-on-one conversation. Michael tells her that he has been suspended for missing too many days of school without an approved excuse. He also tells Ms. Graham that he is always hungry because his mom works all day and does not leave food for them to have upon arrival home. When Ms. Graham asks about his siblings, Michael tells her that they are typically less hungry than him because they are able to eat during school.

Questions

1. What educational story do you imagine is told about Michael?
2. What story do you think is told about Mrs. Graham? About the community she serves? About Mrs. Graham's responsibility to that community?

3. Where in this case are people telling stories (or making judgments) about hard work, perseverance, and success?
4. What other assets (individual and within the community) beyond hard work and perseverance are evident?
5. Think of an educational story that you might tell if we enacted the resources identified in question 4 with a community lens instead of the individual story we see here.

TELLING NEW STORIES

Like our stories, the cases here represent stories we have both heard over and over again when working with preservice and in-service teachers. Because we continue to encounter such cases and such similar educator and student storytelling about the situations and contexts presented here we want and need to tell new and different stories. We also deeply understand how hard it is to "give our imaginations free play" when we are caught up in the meritocratic master narrative that creates binaries where educational systems view identity or what it means to be a "certain kind of person in a given context" (Gee 2001, 99) as fixed. The American story is so pervasive that when stories are pulled up into its framing, we may not even notice. We suggest a few ways to break us all out of the limitations of the hyper-individualized merit narrative and begin to let us tell the stories we aspire to tell.

Reflection/Self Awareness. Educators and other professionals in schools must be aware of how the stories they tell perpetuate inequities. Change starts with self-awareness and we cannot be aware without critical self-reflection. What stories were told to you about hard work and perseverance? How have these stories shaped your understanding of success and excellence?

Sociopolitical Consciousness. Sociopolitical consciousness refers to an individual's ability to critically analyze the political, economic, and social forces shaping society and one's status in it. Where in these stories and your own would it have helped to take up a sociopolitical consciousness? **Culturally Relevant Curriculum.** Changing the curriculum starts with using student culture as the foundation for learning, and promotes the use of students' local and global culture in all aspects of the curriculum design and delivery. Where in these stories and your own did teachers expect the curriculum that reached them to also reach you?

As you move into the final chapter of this text, we once again encourage you to embrace imagination as "the capacity that enables us to move through the barriers of the taken-for- granted and summon up alternative possibilities for living, for being in the world. It permits us to set aside (at least for a while) the stiflingly familiar and the banal. It opens us to visions of the possible rather than the predictable; it permits us, if we choose to give our imaginations free play, to look at things as if they could be otherwise" (Greene 1995, 494).

FIVE
The Stories We Aspire to Tell

NICHELLE'S STORY

The small group of students were gathered in the high school library for the presentation on AP courses. The AP program was a strategic partnership designed to support African American students and students from a poverty context in the county who were underrepresented in advanced placement courses. The grant, given by a local foundation, was used to support innovative, teacher-led projects in secondary schools in six area school districts. The central component of the grant was continuous teacher learning as the foundational element to student success, learning, and achievement (Darling-Hammond 2006, 2008, 2010). Ms. Dawson was in the second year of this county-wide program and she was leading the efforts to increase the number of AP African American students in her high school. She was doing this despite the fact that she was a special education teacher whose job description was to serve as a resource to students with learning and behavioral challenges. Yet, without hesitation, she stepped into this leadership position, which required her to be a part of a professional learning community (PLC), where she would have additional work and responsibilities serving students that she otherwise would not serve. As the only African American teacher in the building, this is what she wanted, to interface with more African American students and to do so for what she considered to be "positive" reasons.

During the first year in the program, her teacher team worked to change school policies related to AP class preparation and enrollment. The team had been assembled by a former principal in the building who had been moved to another building. Prior to her leaving she wrote the grant and encouraged each member to join the team. The principal was strategic, having chosen a veteran guidance counselor, an AP social studies teacher, and Ms. Dawson. The diverse three-member team had differing views of this issue, yet they worked together to address the inequity by completing a comprehensive data analysis that revealed a sizable number of African American students were eligible for Advanced Placement classes, yet were not guided to enroll in the courses. In addition, a sizable disparity was discovered in communication which resulted in White families receiving services and being alerted by school officials prior to enrollment in AP courses. To address this gap in services, the teachers invited over 110 families and eligible students to an information sharing event in the community. It was well attended with over thirty-five families present. Families (many including both parents) attended the initial information session held at a community center in the district. In addition, school counselors and honors teachers began to inform students, especially to all enrollees in the honors classes, who would exit from honors programs and not take Advanced Placement courses in eleventh and twelfth grade years.

Now, during the second year of the program, Ms. Dawson has gathered the students to participate in activities to support their matriculation through the courses. This support included direct contact with faculty from a nearby university. As the faculty member supporting Ms. Dawson's learning, I also made trips to the high school to support the students. This is where I met Nichelle, a senior who, as luck would have it, wanted to be a teacher.

Nichelle, a twelfth-grader, was front and center in the library when I arrived. Four students sat circling her, one of whom was her younger brother. It was clear from their interaction that they were close friends. As the discussion progressed, her leadership skills were evident by her eagerness to answer questions, support her peers, and describe how much she loved her school and the educators who were supporting her. At the end of the discussion, she introduced herself to me by saying that the former principal, Dr. Williams, had told her to reach out to me. "I want to be a teacher and I want to come to your university." "This is great news," I said. "We are always looking for bright students like yourself and the field of education needs more African American teachers." She smiled and said that Dr. Williams told her that and had encouraged her to pursue a degree in education. I asked if she knew that Dr. Williams had been a student of mine. Once again, she smiled. "Yes," she said, "and, I am going to be one, too."

Nichelle did matriculate to our university and we were two of her professors. She took Gretchen's class the very first semester of college and it was evident that the transition was difficult. She went from a schooling context where African Americans were 50 percent of the population and she was viewed as a leader and capable of doing the work to one where she was now 6 percent of the population and questioned. In all of her education courses, she was the only African American student. As the semester progressed, Gretchen did not see the same sparkle in her eyes that she saw when she first met her. Instead, Nichelle "blended in" and was eager to make the twenty-minute trip home every weekend. After each class meeting, Gretchen would approach her to check in. At the end of the semester, Gretchen recommended two professors in the School of Education that Nichelle should take. Amy was one of them.

Today, Nichelle is a senior. She adjusted, academically and socially. She figured out how to become a part of the college scene, having pledged a sorority, and how to stay close to home. She still goes there frequently. She is slated to be a student teacher in the district where she graduated. Dr. Williams made the call to make sure that this happened. It is Dr. Williams thinking that Nichelle will come back home to teach because, "We need her here."

As we reflect on our individual stories and the stories in this research, we wonder what story Nichelle will tell about her success as an African American student from an underserved school district who attended a predominantly White university to become a teacher. Will the story be about her hard work, dedication, and perseverance, the narrative of American individualism and meritocracy? Or, will it be about community and collaboration as evidenced by the work of Dr. Williams, Ms. Dawson, or the countless other invisible people who touched her life? Will she tell stories about the systems and structures she navigated in order to get through high school and college or will they be rendered invisible? In other words, will she teach her students about structural inequities and advocate for students in ways that teach them the skills they need to actually survive unjust academic systems or will she tell them to simply work hard?

We began this journey together because of the similarities in the stories that shaped our lives. The parallels between our cultural narratives of hard work and perseverance are striking despite our different race, age, and regionality. In our conversations, we understood that, despite the differences in our family stories, the spaces where we wanted to create different experiences for students like ourselves has led us to the educational advocacy work we are committed to doing.

It is also the intersections of these differences that made us ask the larger and deeper questions. How did the stories we heard growing up and while in school help us and how did they cause harm? In recognizing that the stories we were told are not benign and neutral in their telling or in how they get picked up, how do we tell complicated, complex stories about success and excellence? How do we tell more complex stories that have the power to transform how we think about what it means to work hard and what it means to persevere? Finally, how might we tell stories that render the collaborative reality of our human existence and the journeys that define our lives in ways that honor our human connectivity? Thinking more deeply, we ask: "How might telling different stories get us closer to creating and ultimately sustaining the equitable educational systems that educators profuse to want?"

We are not surprised that the master narrative of meritocracy has the power that it does and that meritocracy and individual competition, hard work, and perseverance, are centered in schools. We both have school-aged children. Yet, our own individual stories suggest that telling these stories comes at a huge cost. First, we know that few people actually reach the types of success normalized in meritocracy narratives. Second, for those of us who do "make it," the individual act of surviving the meritocracy narrative is palatable because the pain associated with not being "enough" is cumulative and the weight of the undue burden is unsustainable.

To be clear, we value the role of hard work and effort as an important aspect of success. Similarly, we value strategic use of talent. Yet, we have come to recognize that without the skills and tools to critique, navigate, and hopefully, change barriers created by inequities and injustice inherent in our educational policies and procedures—students from a poverty context and students of color are more likely to fail. Failure is all too likely despite their (and our) very best efforts and the efforts schools undertake to recognize and nurture student talents. The same is true for their teachers.

TELLING COMMUNAL STORIES

Few would argue that we live during a time in history where the educational opportunities available to young people are *extraordinarily* inequitable. The US wealth gaps are at an all-time high and educators and students in every setting understand that their success is closely tied to their abilities to either hold on to the privileges they have been afforded or to break into the systems that have denied them. The options for success have been constructed as either/or propositions. How might we break this cycle?

This book is our attempt to better understand how the stories we tell perpetuate educational inequities. We shared our personal educational narratives, we spoke with educators in underserved school districts, and we spoke with their students. We used the American Dream as a merit narrative to ground the history of our educational system as central to building and sustaining hard work and perseverance as a cultural marker for financial and academic success.

In search of ways to be more effective in our own work, we turn to Kumashiro's (2015) work. The educators and students in our research did not question the meritocratic narrative or the value placed on hard work and perseverance in school-based metaphors. Instead, they assumed these traits to be effective strategies for academic success, without questioning systemic and structural barriers that may limit the effectiveness of hard work and perseverance as a means to open opportunities and provide access to the American Dream. Kumashiro argues that in order to challenge what we understand as common sense in schools, we must first reframe our understanding of education. He cites Lakoff to define the impact of frames:

> Frames are mental structures that shape the way we see the world. As a result, they shape the goals we seek, the plans we make, the way we act, and what counts as good or bad outcome of our actions. You can't see or hear frames. They are part of what cognitive scientists call the "cognitive unconscious"—structures in our brains that we cannot consciously access, but know by their consequences: the way we reason and what counts as common sense. We also know frames through language. All words are defined relative to conceptual frames. When you hear a word, its frame (or collection of frames) is activated in your brain. Reframing is changing the way the public sees the world. It is changing what counts as common sense. (Lakoff 2004, p. xv, emphasis in original)

The stories we share here suggest that there is a disconnect between reality and myth in the ways that hard work and perseverance are used as metaphors to frame educational success (Generett & Olson 2020). We come to this conclusion based upon the disconnect between the stories educators tell students, how students take up these stories, and the intended outcomes. Looking specifically at what education says it wants for students, it is abundantly clear that the weight of working hard and persevering, coupled with feelings of isolation and responsibility, has the potential to negatively impact our most vulnerable students. Our most visible example of this is how students in the study describe their peers. In making sense of their contexts, students in this study tell similar deficit stories about their peers as the ones told by outsiders who look down upon their communities.

In oppressive systems this response is not uncommon, and Freire helps us to understand that this response is basic to the relationship between oppressors and the oppressed. He writes,

> One of the basic elements of the relationship between oppressor and oppressed is *prescription*. Every prescription represents the imposition of one individual's choice upon another, transforming the consciousness of the person prescribed to into one that conforms with the prescriber's consciousness. Thus, the behavior of the oppressed is a prescribed behavior, following as it does the guidelines of the oppressor. (Friere 1989, 4)

In this way, we fear we are educating students in low income communities to become oppressors in unjust systems rather than teaching them to transform unjust systems.

It is clear that there is a disconnect between reality and myth in these school-based merit narratives. Educators and students know this. Parents and community members also know this as well. As educational researchers, we believe that additional research is needed to better understand what we can do to assist well-intentioned educators to move away from individual stories to co-created stories that challenge the meritocracy narrative.

We believe that reframing begins by telling stories that develop a critical consciousness that disrupt prescriptive responses. Critical consciousness points to how historically oppressed people interpret and respond to oppressive forces in their contexts (Freire 1989). Dialogical practices that support personal reflection in connection with shared lived experiences allow people to understand how their lives are impacted by social structures (Murray & Milner 2015). If educators are to create the context for collective success for students living in underserved, underresourced districts, then they must also work to reframe the stories they tell about systemic structures that deny their students.

Such change can happen only if we move away from narratives that honor individuals for rising above the system in favor of exploring how communities and groups transform oppressive educational systems. Perhaps we need to support educators' *moral* courage if we are to support them in confronting the familiar narratives of individual meritocracy that pervade schools. If educators are to create the context for collective success for their students, then they must also work to change the stories they tell about systemic structures that deny their students. Similarly, we need to support the development and learning of social critical consciousness in students so they are less likely to pick up these narratives when told them. Such change can happen only if we move away from narratives that honor individuals for rising above the system in favor of exploring how communities and groups transform oppressive educational systems. Educators need to tell collaborative stories that center the collaborative efforts fundamental to success because transformation happens when people work together. If educators work to avoid the meritocracy trap, they will avoid the seductive nature of individual stories that ultimately sustain the powerful narrative of hard work and work ethic. We are products of a collective even when rendered invisible. None of us make it alone.

Bibliography

Bell, Derrick. *Silent Covenants:* Brown v. Board of Education *and the Unfulfilled Hopes for Racial Reform*. Oxford, New York: Oxford University Press, 2005.
Bergin, Daniel and Helen Cooks. "High School Students of Color Talk about Accusations of 'Acting White.'" *The Urban Review* 34, no. 2 (2002): 113–134.
Brantlinger, Ellen A. *Dividing Classes: How the Middle Class Negotiates and Rationalizes School Advantage*. New York: Routledge, 2003.
Britzman, Deborah P. *Practice Makes Practice: A Critical Study of Learning to Teach*. Albany, NY: State University of New York Press, 1990.
Brown v. Board of Educ. 347 U.S. 483 (1954).
Bruner, Jerome. *Acts of Meaning*. Cambridge, MA: Harvard University Press, 1990.
Carter, Dorinda. "Cultivating a Critical Race Consciousness for African American School." *Educational Foundations* Winter-Spring (2008): 11–28.
Caruthers, Loyce. "Using Storytelling to Break the Silence That Binds Us to Sameness in Our Schools." *The Journal of Negro Education* 75, no. 4 (2006): 661–675. Accessed September 8, 2020, http://www.jstor.org/stable/40034665.
"COVID-19 Hospitalization and Death by Race/Ethnicity." Centers for Disease Control and Prevention. https://www.cdc.gov/coronavirus/2019-ncov/covid-data/investigations-discovery/hospitalization-death-by-race-ethnicity.html.
Chapman, Thandeka K. "Interrogating Classroom Relationships and Events: Using Portraiture and Critical Race Theory in Education Research." *Educational Researcher* 36, no. 3 (2007): 156–162.
Chevan, Albert. "The Growth of Home Ownership: 1940–1980." *Demography* 26, no. 2 (1989): 249–266. http://www.jstor.org/stable/2061523.
Coffey, Amanda J. and Paul A. Atkinson. *Making Sense of Qualitative Data: Complementary Research Strategies*. Thousand Oaks, CA: Sage, 1996.
Collins, Patricia and Sirma Bilge. *Intersectionality*. Malden, MA: Polity Press, 2016.
Cook, Daniella and Gretchen Generett. "On the Process of Becoming: Black Women Academics Othermothering From the Margins." In *Queen Mothers: Articulating the Spirit of Black Women Teacher-Leaders*. Edited by Rhonda Jefferies, 117–134. Information Age Publishing. 2019.
Cullen, Jim. *The American Dream: A Short History of an Idea that Shaped American History*. New York: Oxford University Press, 2003.
Darling-Hammond, Linda. "Constructing 21st Century Teacher Education." *Journal of Teacher Education* 57, no. 3 (2006) https://doi.org/10.1177/0022487105285962.
———. "Teacher Education and the American Future." *Journal of Teacher Education* 61, no. 35 (2010).
Darling-Hammond, L., B. Barron, P. D. Pearson, A. H. Schoenfeld, E. K. Stage, T. D. Zimmerman, G. N. Cervetti, and J. L. Tilson. *Powerful Learning: What We Know About Teaching for Understanding*. San Francisco: Jossey-Bass, 2008.
Darder, Antonia. *Culture and Power in the Classroom: A Critical Foundation for Bicultural Education*. New York: Bergin & Garvey, 1991.
Delpit, Lisa. *Other People's Children: Cultural Conflict in the Classroom*. New York: New Press, 2006.
Dewey, John. *Experience and Education*. New York: Macmillan, 1938.
Dillard, Cynthia B. "Walking Ourselves Back Home: The Education of Teachers With/In the World." *Journal of Teacher Education* 53, no. 5 (2002): 383–392.

Duckworth, Angela. *Grit: The Power of Passion and Perseverance*. New York: Scribner, 2016.
Dweck, Carol S. *Mindset: The New Psychology of Success*. New York: Random House, 2006.
Dyson, Anne H. and Cecila Genishi. *The Need for Story: Cultural Diversity in Classroom and Community*. Urbana, IL: National Council of Teachers of English, 1994.
Erikson, Erik. *Identity: Youth and Crisis*. New York: Norton, 1968.
Farmer, Ruth. "Place but Not Importance: The Race for Inclusion in the Academe. In *Spirit, Space, and Survival: African American Women in (White) Academe*. Edited by Joy James and Ruth Farmer, 196–217. Routledge Press, 1993.
Francis, Dania and Christian E. Weller. "The Black-White Wealth Gap Will Widen Educational Disparities During the Coronavirus Pandemic." Center for American Progress, August 12, 2020. https://www.americanprogress.org/issues/race/news/2020/08/12/489260/black-white-wealth-gap-will-widen-educational-disparities-coronavirus-pandemic/.
Freire, Paulo. *The Pedagogy of the Oppressed*. New York: Continuum Press, 1989.
Fullan, Michael. *Change Forces: Probing the Depth of Educational Reform*. School Development and Management Series: 10. Falmer Press, 1993.
GALEWiLL Center for Opportunity and Progress, and Public Agenda (2012). *The Invisible Dream*. Retrieved from https://www.publicagenda.org/pages/the-invisible-dream.
Gee, James. "Identity as an Analytic Lens for Research in Education." *Review of Research in Education* 25 (2001): 99–125.
Generett, Gretchen and Amy Olson. "The Stories We Tell: How Merit Narratives Undermine Success for Urban Youth." *Urban Education* 55, no. 3 (2020): 394–423.
Generett, Gretchen and Sheryl Cozart. "The Spirit Bears Witness: Reflections of Two African American Women's Journey in the Academy." *NER* 62, no. 62 (2011): 141–165.
Generett, Gretchen and Mark Hicks. "Beyond Reflective Competency: Teaching for Audacious Hope in Action." *Journal of Transformative Education* 2, no. 3 (2004): 187–203.
Giroux, Henry. *Border Crossings: Cultural Workers and the Politics of Education*. New York: Routledge Press, 2004.
Giroux, Henry. *Teachers as Intellectuals: Towards a Critical Pedagogy of Learning*. New York: Bergin & Garvey, 1988.
Glaser, Barney and Anselm Strauss. *The Discovery of Grounded Theory: Strategies for Qualitative Research*. Hawthorne, NY: Aldine Press, 1967.
Goldenberg, Ira. *Oppression and Social Intervention*. Chicago: Nelson-Hall, 1978.
Goldstein, Dana. *The Teacher Wars: A History of America's Most Embattled Profession*. New York: Penguin Random House, 2014.
Gorski, Paul. "Poverty and the Ideological Imperative: A Call to Unhook from Deficit and Grit Ideology and to Strive for Structural Ideology in Teacher Education." *Journal of Education for Teaching* 42 (2016): 378–386.
Grantham, Tarek and Donna Ford. "Providing Access for Culturally Diverse Gifted Students: From Deficit to Dynamic Thinking." *Theory into Practice* 42, no. 3 (2003): 217–225.
Greene, Maxine. *Releasing the Imagination: Essays on Education, the Arts, and Social Change*: San Francisco: Jossey-Bass, 1995.
Guajardo, Miguel, Francisco Guajardo, Christopher Janson, and Matthew Militello. *Reframing Community Partnerships in Education: Uniting the Power of Place and Wisdom of People*. New York: Routledge, 2015.
Halverson, Jeffry, H. L. Goodall, and Steven Corman. *Master Narratives of Islamist Extremism*. New York: Palgrave Macmillan. 2011.
Heidegger, Martin. *Being and Time*. Oxford: Blackwell Publishing, 1962.
Hendrickson, Roberta. "Remembering the Dream: Alice Walker, Meridian and the Civil Rights Movement." *Melus* 24, no. 3 (1999): 111–128.

Hicks, Mark and Gretchen Generett. "Barriers to Transformative Collaboration for Justice within Cross-Cultural Communities." In *Handbook of Research on the Social Foundations of Education*. Edited by Stephen Tozer, Annette Henry, Bernardo Gallegos, and Paula Price, 684–697. Lawrence Erlbaum & Associates Press, 2011

Hochschild, Arlie. *The Second Shift and the Revolution at Home*. London, England: Penguin Press, 1989.

Hurston, Zora. *Their Eyes Were Watching God*. New York: Harper Perennial, 1998.

James, Joy. "African Philosophy, Theory, and 'Living Thinkers.'" In *Spirit, Space, and Survival: African American Women in (White) Academe*. Edited by Joy James and Ruth Farmer, 31–47. New York: Routledge Press, 1993.

Jeffrey, Julie. *Education for Children of the Poor: A Study of the Origins and Implementation of the Elementary and Secondary Education Act of 1965*. Columbus: Ohio State University Press, 1978.

Katznelson, Ira. *When Affirmative Action was White: An Untold History of Racial Inequality in Twentieth-Century America*. New York: W.W. Norton, 2005.

Kendi, Ibram X. *Stamped from the Beginning: The Definitive History of Racist Ideas in America*. New York: Bold Type Books, 2017.

Kim, Yong-Chen and Sandra Ball-Rokeach. "Community Storytelling Network, Neighborhood Context, and Civic Engagement: A Multilevel Approach." *Human Communication Research* 32 (2006): 411–439.

Koerner, Melissa. "Courage as Identity Work: Accounts of Workplace Courage." *The Academy of Management Journal* 57, no. 1 (2014): 63–93.

Kumashiro, Kevin. *Against Common Sense: Teaching and Learning Toward Social Justice*. New York: Routledge Press, 2015.

Kumashiro, Kevin. *The Seduction of Common Sense: How the Right has Framed the Debate on America's Schools*. New York: Teachers College Press, 2008.

Kumashiro, Kevin. "Toward a Theory of Anti-Oppressive Education." *Review of Educational Research* 70 (2000): 25–53.

Ladson-Billings, Gloria and William F. Tate IV. "Toward a Critical Race Theory of Education." *Teachers College Record* 97, no. 1 (1995): 47–68.

Lakoff, George. *Don't Think of an Elephant: Know Your Values and Frame the Debate*. White River Junction, VT: Chelsea Green Publishing Company, 2003.

Lakoff, George and Mark Johnson. *Metaphors We Live By*. Chicago: University of Chicago Press, 2003.

Leggo, Carl. "Writing Truth in Classrooms: Personal Revelation and Pedagogy." *International Journal of Whole Schooling* 3, no. 1 (2007): 27–37.

Liu, Amy. "Unraveling the Myth of Meritocracy Within the Context of US Higher Education." *Higher Education* 62 (2011): 383–397.

Loose, Florence. "Individualism: Valued Differently by Parents and Teachers of Primary, Junior High, and High School Students." *Social Psychology of Education* 11 (2008): 117–131.

Luttrell, Wendy. "The Two-in-Oneness of Class." In *The Way Class Works: Readings on School, Family, and the Economy*. Edited by Lois Weis, 60–76. New York: Routledge Press, 2008.

Marshall, Catherine and Gretchen Rossman. *Designing Qualitative Research*. Thousand Oaks, CA: Sage, 2006.

Mayer, Frederick W. *Narrative Politics Stories and Collective Action*. New York: Oxford University Press, 2014.

McAdams, Dan P. *The Redemptive Self: Stories Americans Live By*. New York: Oxford University Press, 2006.

McIntosh, Peggy. "White Privilege: Unpacking the Invisible Knapsack." In *Re-Visioning Family Therapy: Race, Culture, and Gender in Clinical Practice*. Edited Monica McGoldrick, 147–152. The Guilford Press, 1998.

———. *White Privilege and Male Privilege: A Personal Account of Coming to See Correspondences Through Work in Women's Studies*. Wellesley, MA: Wellesley College, Center for Research on Women, 1988.

Mehan, Hugh, Lea Hubbard, and Irene Villanueva. "Forming Academic Identities: Accommodation Without Assimilation Among Involuntary Minorities." *Anthropology and Education Quarterly* 25, no. 2 (1994): 91–117.
Mettler, Suzanne. "How the G.I. Bill Built the Middle Class and Enhanced Democracy." *Scholars Strategy Network Key Findings* (2012).
Milner, H. Richard. "Disrupting Deficit Notions of Difference: Counter-Narratives of Teachers and Community in Urban Education." *Teaching and Teacher Education* 24 (2008): 1573–1598.
Mishler, Elliot G. "Models of Narrative Analysis: A Typology." *Journal of Narrative and Life History* 5 (1995): 87–123.
Morrison, Toni. "'I Wanted to Carve Out a World Both Culture Specific and Race-Free': An Essay by Toni Morrison." (2019). Retrieved from https://www.theguardian.com/books/2019/aug/08/toni-morrison-rememory-essay.
Murray, Ira and H. Richard Milner. "Toward a Pedagogy of Sociopolitical Consciousness in Outside of School Programs." *Urban Review* 47, no. 5 (2015): 893–913. Doi:10.1007/s11256-015-0339-4.
National Civil Rights Museum at the Lorraine Hotel (2014). *Courage in the Civil Rights Movement: A Resource for Educators*. Retrieved from https://www.civilrightsmuseum.org/educators.
Newman, Katherine S. *Falling from Grace: Downward Mobility in the Age of Affluence*. Berkeley: University of California Press, 1988.
Oakes, Jeanie. *Keeping Track: How Schools Structure Inequality*. New Haven, CT: Yale University Press, 2005.
Oyserman, Daphna, Larry Gant, and Joel Ager. "A Socially Contextualized Model of African American Identity: Possible Selves and School Persistence." *Journal of Personality and Social Psychology* 69 (1995): 1216–1232.
Perry, T., C. Steele, and A. G. Hilliard. *Young, Gifted, and Black: Promoting High Achievement among African-American Students*. Boston: Beacon Press, 2003.
Piercy, Marge. *Circles on the Water: Selected Poems by Marge Piercy*. New York: Alfred A. Knopf Doubleday Publishing, 1982.
Press, Eyal. *Beautiful Souls: The Courage and Conscience of Ordinary People in Extraordinary Times*. New York: Picador First Edition, 2012.
Press, Eyal. "Moral Courage: A Sociological Perspective." *Society* 55, no. 2 (2018): 181–192.
Riesman, David. *The Lonely Crowd: A Study of the Changing American Character*. New Haven, CT: Yale University Press, 1961.
Ris, Ethan W. "Grit: A Short History of a Useful Concept." *Journal of Educational Controversy* 10, no. 1 (2015): 1–18.
Sandlin, Jennifer and M. Carolyn Clark. "From Opportunity to Responsibility: Political Master Narratives, Social Policy, and Success Stories in Adult Literacy Education." *Teacher College Record* 111 (2009): 999–1029.
Scott, J. and D. Leonhardt. "Shadowy Lines that Still Divide." *New York Times*. Retrieved from http://www.nytimes.com/pages/national/class/index.html.
Senge, Peter. *The Fifth Discipline: The Art and Practice of the Learning Organization*. New York: Doubleday Currency Publishing Group, 1990.
Smith, Jonathan, Paul Flowers, and Michael Larkin. *Interpretative Phenomenological Analysis: Theory, Method and Research*. Thousand Oaks, CA: Sage Publications, 2009.
Townes, Emilie M. "Ethics as an Art of Doing: The Work Our Souls Must Have." In *The Acts of Ministry: Feminist-Womanist Approaches*. Edited by Christie Cozard Neuger, 143–61. Westminster John Knox Press, 1996.
Trumbull, Elise, Carrie Rothstein-Fisch, and Elvia Hernandez. "Parent Involvement—According to Whose Values?" *School Community Journal* 13, no. 2 (2003): 45–72.
Ullici, Kerri and Tyrone Howard. "Pathologizing the Poor: Implications for Preparing Teachers to Work in High-Poverty Schools." *Urban Education* 50, no. 2 (March 2015): 170–193.
Wade-Gayles, Gloria. *Anointed to Fly*. New York: Harlem River Press, 1991.

Weber, Max. *The Protestant Ethic and the Spirit of Capitalism*. New York: Scribner, 1958.
Weis, Lois. *The Way Class Works: Readings on School, Family, and the Economy*. New York: Routledge, 2008.
Yosso, Tara J. "Whose Culture has Capital? A Critical Race Theory Discussion of Community Cultural Wealth" *Race Ethnicity and Education* 8, no. 1 (2005): 69–91.
Young, Michael. *The Rise of the Meritocracy*. New Brunswick, NJ: Transaction Publishers, 2011.

Index

Adams, 29
advocacy, 5
advocacy and navigation, 67–68; "family meetings" in, 44; power differentials in, 44; in stories educators tell, 43–44; "Trigger Wall" in, 43–44
African Americans, 58, 68; AP Program for, 85–86; Black History Month, 67–68, 79–80; leadership skills of, 86; PLC and, 85–86. *See also* Generett, Gretchen Givens
Alger, Jr., Horatio, 18, 52, 53
Amy. *See* Olson, Amy
AP history exams, 77
AP program, 85–86
athletics, 62, 80

back story, 2–3; moral courage and storytelling, 3–6
Bilge, Sirma, 14
Black History Month, 67–68, 79–80
Black teachers, 13, 74–76. *See also specific teachers*
Brantlinger, Ellen A., 33
Britzman, Deborah P., 22
Brown v Board of Education, 32
"But I'm an ally," 76; AP history exams in, 77; classroom "politics" in, 77; equity work in, 76–77; immigration in, 77; questions on, 78

capitalism, 28
Carter, Dorinda, 55
Caruthers, Loyce, 4, 22
Center for American Progress, x
Center for Race and Social Problems, ix
charter schools, 75
civil rights, 4, 8, 10, 79–80
classroom "politics," 77

classroom space, 48–49
"cognitive unconscious," 89
Cole, Johnnetta, 12
collective action, 49–50
collective narrative, 15
collective story, 72–73. *See also* stories, reframing
Collins, Patricia, 14
common sense, 56–58. *See also* repetition and negative implications of "common sense"
communal stories, 88; frames in, 88–89; oppressors in, 89, 90; reframing in, 90
communities, 11, 21–22; Mayer on, 72–73; for Nichelle, 86–87; PLC, 85–86
Community Learning Exchange, ix
competition, 20, 33, 78
Corman, Steven, 25
courage, 23; from achievements, 45–47, 46; in advocacy without navigation, 67–68; collective action in, 49–50; beyond expectations in, 47–49; moral, 3–6, 24; perseverance and, 40, 42, 48, 62; professional, 47–50; in responsibility and isolation, 65–66
COVID-19, ix, x. *See also* "Is the pandemic really that awful?"
Cozart, Sheryl Conrad, 15
Crawford, Ramona, 80–82
critical race theory (CRT), 31, 68
culturally relevant curriculum, 82
culture, community, 72–73

Delpit, Lisa, 14
Dillard, Cynthia, 17
Dweck, Carol S., 53

educator fatigue, 74–75, 76

97

educators, 34, 36–38; White men as, 46–47. *See also* stories educators tell

educators' themes, 38. *See also* advocacy and navigation; hard work and perseverance; identifying and supporting individual talent; protection

effort, 5, 21, 26, 28, 32, 34; school stories of, 34–35, 46, 53, 54, 56, 59

Elementary and Secondary Education Act (ESEA), 30–31

English teacher, 79–80

equity, 24, 33, 75, 76; back story of, 2–3; COVID-19 related to, x; growth mindset and, 53–54; race and, 30, 44; students in poverty and, 1, 33, 52–53, 55

equity work, 76–77

Erikson, Erik, 66

ESEA. *See* Elementary and Secondary Education Act

everyday functioning, 26

expectations, 27, 39, 76–77; going beyond, 24, 47–49, 59, 60, 61–62; in "Is this the best I can do?," 75–76

failure, 20

"Faking it until you make it": ambitions in, 78; anxiety in, 78; competition in, 78; extracurriculars in, 78; hard work and perseverance in, 78; questions on, 79

family stories, 87; in Olson's narrative, 18–19, 21

frames, 88–89

Freire, Paulo, 89

generativity, 31, 34, 36, 56, 60; in Generett's narrative, being the bridge, 6–7, 8–10, 13

Generett, Gretchen, 5, 86

Generett's narrative, 2, 6, 21

Generett's narrative, being the bridge, 6, 8; generativity in, 6–7, 8–10, 13; modeling in, 7–8; redemptive narratives in, 9–10

Generett's story, building the bridge: cross-cultural communities in, 11; hope in, 11; race in, 11–12; teenage years in, 10, 12; uplift suasion in, 11–12

Generett's story, walking the bridge, 17; claim your space in, 16–17; college faculty in, 14–17; intersectionality in, 14, 16; marginalization in, 14–15; scholarship in, 15

gifted program, 20

Goodall, H. L., 25

Gorski, Paul, 52

Graphic Design, 73, 74

Great Depression, 28–29

Greene, Maxine, 22

Gretchen. *See* Generett, Gretchen Givens

grit, 52–53

growth mindset, 53–54

Guajardo, Francisco, 36

Guajardo, Miguel, 36

guidance counselor, 73–74

Guy-Sheftall, Beverly, 13, 14

Halverson, Jeffry, 25

hard work, 8, 27, 35, 68; in Olson's narrative, 19–20, 20–21; in school accountability, 31–32

hard work and perseverance, 26, 27, 45–47, 52, 80, 87; age discrimination in, 41; in athletics, 62; courage in, 60, 61–62; in educators' themes, 38–42; in "Faking it until you make it," 78; Graphic Design related to, 73, 74; for high achievers, 56; inspiration in, 40–41, 42; mentorship in, 62–63; meritocratic values in, 40–41; neighborhood violence and, 39; of Nichelle, 86–87; obstacles in, 38–39; responsibility and isolation in, 63–66; in stories educators tell, 38–42; in stories students tell, 57–58, 60–63; "success" stories in, 39–40; in "What about me?," 73, 74

Hicks, Mark, 11

Hilliard, A. G., 69

history teacher, 76–77

Hughes, Langston, 29–30

hunger, 81

Hutchinson, 4–5

hyper-individualism, 39, 56, 68, 72; in school accountability, 33, 34; in U.S. meritocracy: master narrative, 27, 28

identifying and supporting individual talent: inequities in, 43; in stories educators tell, 42–43
identities, 1, 54, 58, 60, 66, 68
imagination, 82
immigration, 77
individualism, 27. *See also* hyper-individualism
individual's journey line, 25–26
individual stories, 71, 74; master narratives compared to, 25
inquiry, 22
intersectionality, 14
invisibility, 20
"Is the pandemic really that awful?": athletics in, 80; hard work and perseverance in, 80; hunger in, 81; online learning in, 80–81; questions on, 81–82; suspension in, 81
"Is this the best I can do?": accountability in, 75; educator fatigue in, 74–75, 76; expectations in, 75–76; lead teacher in, 76; questions on, 76

James, Joy, 7
Janson, Christopher, 36
Johnson, Lyndon B., 30, 31
Johnson, Mark, 26
journey lines, 25–26, 58–59; in stories educators tell, 24, 35–36, 37

Kendi, Ibram X., 11–12
King, Martin Luther, Jr., 79
knowledge, 22
Koerner, Melissa, 3
Kumashiro, Kevin, 55, 56–57, 88–89

Ladson-Billings, Gloria, 14
Lakoff, George, 26, 88–89
Leggo, Carl, 4–5
Liu, Olson, 33, 58
Loose, Florence, 34
Luttrell, Wendy, 56

marginalization, 21–22
master narratives, 25, 88; repetition and negative implications of "common sense" and, 55–57; of White men, 24–25
mathematics, 20
math teacher, 74–76
Mayer, Frederick, 72–73
McAdams, Dan P., 6–7, 10, 25, 26, 28, 36
memories, 17, 23
mentorship, 62–63
meritocracy, 68, 72; courage and, 5; myth of, 1, 5, 26–27, 31
meritocratic myths and school discourse, 51–52, 54–55; growth mindset in, 53–54
Mettler, Suzanne, 29
Militello, Matthew, 36
Milner, H. Richard, 37, 58
Mishler, Elliot G., 24
moral courage, 3–6, 24, 90
Morrison, Toni, 16, 17
"most livable city," ix

narratives, 1
narratives in politics, 72–73
Nichelle: in AP program, 86; community for, 86–87; hard work and perseverance of, 86–87; in University, 86–87
No Child Left Behind (2001), 32
non-conformism, 3

Oakes, Jeanie, 54
Olson, Amy, 2, 5
Olson's narrative, 18, 21; family stories in, 18–19, 21; hard work in, 19–21
online learning, x, 80–81
oppressors, 89

parties, 65
Perry, T., 69
perseverance, 1, 62; courage and, 40, 42, 48, 62; racism and, 55–56; stereotypes and, 41. *See also* hard work and perseverance
PLC. *See* professional learning community

politics, narratives in, 72–73
portraiture, 31
predominantly White institutions (PWI), 15
Prefontaine, Steve, 20
professional learning community (PLC), 85–86
protection: from physical dangers, 44; trust as, 44–45
PWI. *See* predominantly White institutions

qualitative research, 2, 3, 24, 37

racism, ix; perseverance and, 55–56; school accountability and, 31, 32; in U.S. meritocracy: master narrative, 29–30; in "What should I do?," 80
reciprocity, 4–5
The Redemptive Self (McAdams), 10
"redemptive self" narrative, 25
reflection/self awareness, 82
repetition and negative implications of "common sense," 56; master narrative and, 55–57
responsibility and isolation: courage in, 65–66; in hard work and perseverance, 63–66; role models in, 63–65
return to courage, 47–50
Ris, Ethan W., 52
role models, 64–65; for younger siblings, 63–64

school accountability, 30, 75; competition in, 33; CRT in, 31; ESEA in, 30–31; hard work in, 31–32; hyper-individualism in, 33, 34; inequities in, 33; No Child Left Behind in, 32; racism and, 31, 32
Senge, Peter, 8
social justice, 76–77
socio-political consciousness, 82
Spelman College, 12, 16
Steele, C., 69
STEM education, 78
stories. *See specific topics*
stories, reframing: "But I'm an ally," 76–78; challenges in, 71; collective story in, 72–73; "Faking it until you make it," 78–79; "Is the pandemic really that awful?," 80–82; "Is this the best I can do?," 74–76; success stories in, 71; telling new stories in, 82; "What about me?," 73–74; "What should I do?," 79–80
stories as windows of possibility, 21–22
stories educators tell: advocacy and navigation in, 43–44; conclusions and implications on, 45–47, 46; courage in, 23; hard work and perseverance in, 38–42, 45–46; hard work in, 35; identifying and supporting individual talent in, 42–43; journey lines in, 24, 35–36, 37; local heroes in, 34; memories in, 23; meritocracy in, 23–24; methodology in, 35–36; moral courage and, 24; myth in, 34–35; protection in, 44–45; return to courage in, 47–50; stories students tell compared to, 68; "story of us" in, 36; storytelling context in, 35. *See also* school accountability; U.S. meritocracy: master narrative
stories students tell: context of, 57–59; hard work and perseverance in, 57–58, 60–63; journey lines and interviews in, 58–59; meritocratic myths and school discourse related to, 51–55; repetition and negative implications of "common sense" and, 55–57; responsibility and isolation in, 63–65; stories educators tell compared to, 68; students in, 58
stories students tell, analysis, 59; advocacy without navigation in, 67–68; hard work and perseverance in, 60–63; responsibility and isolation in, 63–66; themes in, 60–68
stories we aspire to tell, 85–88; AP program in, 85–86; communal stories in, 88–90; Nichelle in, 86–87
storytelling, 4
storytelling self, 4
students in poverty, 1, 33, 52–53, 55, 81, 85
students of color, 1, 35, 36, 55, 58, 68, 88
"success" stories, 39–40

suicide, 20
suspension, 81
systemic issues, 22

teachers. *See* educators
telling new stories, 82; imagination in, 82; reflection/self awareness in, 82; socio-political consciousness in, 82
timing, 68–69
Tocqueville, Alexis de, 27–28, 29, 33
"Trigger Wall," 43–44
trust, 44–45

University of North Carolina at Chapel Hill, 14
U.S. meritocracy: master narrative: class mobility and economic prosperity in, 27–30; everyday functioning in, 26; Great Depression in, 28–29; hyper-individualism in, 27, 28; master narratives in, 24–25; meaning making in, 25–26; meritocracy in, 26–27; myth of, 26–27; obstacles in, 26; racism in, 29–30; "redemptive self" narrative in, 25; school accountability in, 30–34; sense making in, 25;

Tocqueville and, 27–28, 29

voices, 22

Wade-Gayles, Gloria, 13, 16
Walker, Alice, 13
Weber, Max, 27
"What about me?," 73, 74; hard work and perseverance in, 73, 74; questions on, 74; requirements in, 74; special talent in, 73, 74
"What should I do?," 79; Black History Month in, 79–80; King in, 79; modern Civil Rights source in, 79–80; questions on, 80; racism in, 80
White men, 29; as educators, 46–47; master narrative of, 24–25
White privilege, 33, 47, 52, 55, 76–77
Wilder, Laura Ingalls, 18

younger siblings: in responsibility and isolation, 64; in what about me?, 73, 74

About the Author

Gretchen Givens Generett, PhD, is interim dean and professor in the School of Education at Duquesne University. She is also the Noble J. Dick Endowed Chair in community outreach. She is a qualitative researcher whose research centers educational stories that have been rendered invisible. Her scholarship intermingles traditional sociology of education, African American studies, and feminist studies with more progressive concepts of justice that examine agency, empowerment, and action. In teaching, Gretchen offers stories as a place for students to recast their individual stories to form a collective narrative that can be used as a catalyst for transformation. Her research and teaching suggest that reflective and interactive storytelling serve a function in uncovering and recovering our individual and collective stories so that we can be intentional in our efforts to dismantle systemic inequities.

Amy M. Olson, PhD, is an associate professor of educational psychology and classroom assessment in the Department of Educational Foundations and Leadership at Duquesne University. As a scholar, she examines the equity implications of teachers' beliefs about academic content and learning (both their own and their students). At the heart of all of her work is an exploration of what it means to be successful in the classroom. Amy considers herself a teacher scholar and is intentional about engaging with scholarship that informs her pedagogy. She teaches in undergraduate and graduate teacher education and educational leadership programs with the goal of supporting and sustaining the work of justice-oriented educators.

www.ingramcontent.com/pod-product-compliance
Lightning Source LLC
Chambersburg PA
CBHW020129010526
44115CB00008B/1041